Book 3

Angels, Horses and Other Worldly Lessons

Written and Illustrated by
Kimberly Wickham

Order this book online at www.trafford.com/08-1499
or email orders@trafford.com

Most Trafford titles are also available at major online book retailers.

Note for Librarians: A cataloguing record for this book is available from Library
and Archives Canada at www.collectionscanada.ca/amicus/index-e.html

Printed in Victoria, BC, Canada.

ISBN: 978-1-4251-9153-5 (soft)
ISBN: 978-1-4251-9155-9 (ebook)

 www.trafford.com

North America & international
toll-free: 1 888 232 4444 (USA & Canada)
phone: 250 383 6864 ♦ fax: 250 383 6804 ♦ email: info@trafford.com

<u>Other books by Kimberly Wickham:</u>

Angels and Horses

Summer of Magic Horses

www.kimberlywickham.com

**To:
Judith**

Many thanks for the

editorial help and conversations from
Lisa Palazzolo and Kenlin Wilder;

and lively, involved discussions from Suzanne
Beaumont and Michele Bradbeer.

Chapter 1

Tina was bored. School was always like this, it seemed. She glanced over at Chucky who was busy making teeny little paper airplanes out of his math notebook paper. He carefully folded the pieces tucked away under the desk top, out of the teacher's sight. The lesson going on was a question and answer lesson on social studies having to do with early United States history, a subject which Tina was interested in, but if there were any way to make an interesting subject boring, it was sure to happen at school.

She turned her attention to the birds sitting on the windowsill who were busying themselves by picking at some seeds having fallen from a nearby tree. Tina wondered what they were thinking about or if they were talking to each other. She would have to ask Chucky later. How amazed she was when she learned he could tell what animals were thinking! At first he had seemed reluctant to tell anyone about the great gift he had, but now he was very open about it with her and she loved the way he would matter-of-factly report what any animal they happened upon was thinking. It surprised her what a wonderful sense of humor some of them had.

Tina let her mind drift to their Camp Tarigo experiences of a few weeks ago and how her friendship with Chucky had developed there. Besides her having taught him to ride horses and his having taught her to begin to sense animals, Chucky had met the friends Tina had in the 'other world' school. He had been so surprised when her friends drifted in out of thin air at the barn that rainy evening. Since then, Tina had talked about her adventures with her angel, Marguerite, and the 'other world' a great deal with Chucky. He had even met Marguerite, who had been with Tina quite continuously over the last several months, having first appeared to her during the winter when her mother had been so ill.

Tina brought her attention back into the room and began to think about stopping time and stepping out across the Cosmic Lattice she had become very familiar with as a means of traveling between worlds. She wondered if she were to signal Marguerite in some way if the angel would come to help her travel. Instantly at the moment of that thought the room became completely still and the teacher stopped talking in mid sentence. Chucky looked up abruptly from building paper airplanes, having noticed the sudden silence.

At first he said nothing, but looked around the room, marveling at how the other students and the teacher looked like manikins. He was no longer surprised at the odd occurrences that sometimes took shape around Tina ever since that evening in the barn at camp when her friends arrived on horseback out of thin air. He got up and circled the room, moving between desks and looking closely at one of the students. He walked up to Marly, who was sitting at her desk, staring straight ahead with a bored expression on her face, her chin in her hand. He bent down to look directly into her face and promptly stuck his tongue out.

"There!" he said decidedly. "Turned to stone by your own rotten personality! This is the best you've ever been – completely quiet and unable to move!" Chucky disliked Marly more than most people he had ever met, especially after she had blasted him in the face with the broom polo ball at camp, knocking him clear off his seat. The action probably stung his pride more than it had his face.

"She's not so bad, Chucky," Tina said, getting up from her seat and moving over to where he was hovering over Marly. "She just has trouble getting along with people."

"I'll say! How can anyone get along with someone so creepy? I think she is evil. Does she get along with anyone?" Chucky asked.

"I get along with her okay because I ignore the things I don't like about her and focus instead on the things I do like. Did you ever notice

2

how you can change the way people are towards you by changing the way you see them?" Tina asked.

"What are you talking about?" Chucky replied.

"Well, I mean when you don't react to something a person does if you don't like it, they stop doing it," she answered. "When Marly was being bratty to me at camp I kept changing the subject to something I knew she would be interested in and cheerful about."

"Yeah? Like what?" Chucky asked.

"Well, like talking about her! I knew she made a great Class President so we talked about that instead of the things she didn't like. It worked great!" Tina replied, feeling quite proud of herself that she had figured out how to make Marly easier to get along with. Truth was, for some reason she actually liked some things about Marly. "After changing the subject a few times, I found that Marly stopped attacking me altogether. Sometimes she says things that most people wouldn't say, but most of the time she is nice to me," she added.

"I'll take your word for it, but I'm just going to stay clear of her!" Chucky stated firmly, moving over towards the window where the birds had been eating moments before.

Tina looked around for Marguerite but still there was no sign of her, even though time had stopped and that usually preceded a visit from the angel.

"I have an idea, Chucky," Tina said, as she settled her eyes on the lawn outside the classroom window. "Let's go outside and see if we can find the Cosmic Lattice. We might as well do something fun since time has stopped here!"

"Yeah! Let's go!" Chucky answered, all excited. Tina had told Chucky about the Cosmic Lattice and how she and the others had ridden across it with her angel between worlds. He had been waiting anxiously for a chance to see it for himself.

They left the classroom, making their way out of the building and into the yard where Tina had first discovered that time could stop. She wondered why Marguerite had yet to appear to guide her to the 'other world', but she figured they might be able to find the way themselves. Tina was becoming more and more confident about her ability to control things around her. Her angel had shown her that she, like everyone

3

else, was capable of creating whatever she wanted. All she had to do was to decide and stay focused on it. People were wizards according to Marguerite, and at the 'other world' school the students had always known this. That was the very thing that made it so much fun to visit there. If the children wanted something, they merely created it. No need to wonder whether or not they could do or have something; they *knew* they could!

"Look at this, Chucky. This is where we can step through," Tina said, motioning to the opening in the fence where she had followed the orange cat several months ago. She had still not told him about her experience last winter when she had met Chucky as a grown man and also as a cat. Tina found it difficult to explain how a person could be himself as a kid, himself as a grown-up and himself as a cat, all at the same time. Maybe it would be better left to Marguerite to explain it to Chucky some time.

All at once Tina felt a thickness in the air in front of her. She reached for Chucky's hand and pulled him up next to her, then stepped through the thickness as if stepping through a doorway. Where they had just been disappeared behind them, and in front lay the Cosmic Lattice, buzzing and stretching out as far as they could see.

"Here it is!" exclaimed Tina.

"What is this exactly? Where are we? Where's home... what...?" Chucky said nervously, looking back from where they had just come.

"It's okay. We can get back any time we want to. If we follow this for a while we will get to the 'other world'. This is the Cosmic Lattice I keep telling you about. Listen to it hum. Isn't it beautiful?" Tina asked.

"Yeah, it's cool!" Chucky acknowledged. They walked along for some time in silence, enjoying the floating feeling as they glided effortlessly across the Lattice. "This is really cool!" he exclaimed.

"I like it, too. Marguerite says we can travel to the 'other world' without it but it's more fun this way," Tina answered.

Suddenly, they were at the large field across which they could see the open classroom building where Tina had learned her first lessons in quantum physics. She recollected learning that the universe is made up of energy and everything it contains is just energy vibrating at different speeds.

4

Onyx, the big, black horse Tina and the other children had created by drawing in the air with their fingers operating like magic pens, came galloping across the field.

"Hi, Onyx!" Tina exclaimed.

"He says, 'Hi'… and he asks us if we want a ride to the school…" Chucky reported, reading Onyx's thought.

"Sure," Tina answered happily. She thought the horse was one of the nicest horses she had met. He always seemed kind and willing when ridden by Tina and Marguerite. Tina hopped up first, tightly taking hold of his mane at the withers so she could jump onto his back, and then she helped Chucky climb up behind her.

They trotted across the field towards the school and Jiankara was the first to see them arrive. "Tina!" she called, excitedly, "Come on in! Hi, Chucky!"

The other children jumped up from the circle of hay bales on which they had been sitting and came to greet Tina and Chucky.

Mr. Pierce, the 'assistant' for the group, came over as Tina and Chucky climbed down from Onyx's back. "Welcome, Tina. This must be Chucky, then?" he asked while reaching to shake Chucky's hand.

"Hi, Mr. Pierce. Yes, this is Chucky. Chucky, this is Mr. Pierce. He is sort of like the teacher here," Tina explained.

"How do you do, Sir?" Chucky said politely, shaking the assistant's hand.

"No need to be formal here, Chucky. Come on in and join us. We were just having a little discussion about wave potential here," Mr. Pierce replied, putting one arm around Tina's shoulders and the other around Chucky's to lead them into the circle of hay bales. Chucky had no idea what the assistant was talking about.

Everybody took their places on the bales, Tina and Chucky settling themselves between Jiankara and Ben on one of the larger ones. Chucky looked at Tina nervously but was quickly reassured by her smile and obvious comfort with the people in the group. He felt quite out of place here but decided this kind of classroom seemed a lot more comfortable than the one they had just left. At least here the atmosphere was more relaxed.

"It's okay, Chucky," Tina reassured in a whisper. "These are the coolest kids and Mr. Pierce is called 'an assistant' because he helps them learn stuff instead of just telling them stuff." Chucky nodded showing he understood what she meant.

"Right then, my friends," he said, smiling at Tina and Chucky. "We were discussing energy again. Tina, remember when we were discussing how everything is made up of energy, how everything that seems solid is simply sub-atomic particles or 'energy packets' flashing in and out of a space where we think we see the object appearing?" asked Mr. Pierce.

"Yes, I remember, Mr. Pierce," Tina replied.

"Well, we were just taking that discussion a little further," he continued. "These clusters of energy are more like waves of possibility until we turn our attention to them. Then they become particles vibrating to make up the object we decide to see."

"So any little wave can become anything we want as soon as we look at it?" asked Ben.

"Yes, Ben. This all happens with such lightning speed we don't realize we are doing it at all," Mr. Pierce answered. "Let's play a game. I am going to slow down time and space to show you what happens. Watch this…"

Mr. Pierce stood up and illustrated a chair with his finger acting as a pen. The chair floated in the air just above the floor. "Everybody can see this chair, right?" he asked. Everyone nodded in agreement. "Right. Now, everyone look over at Onyx," he said, indicating the big, black horse grazing just outside the open classroom. Everyone's attention turned to Onyx and immediately they noticed something odd. From the corner of their eyes they could see the chair collapse into little waves of energy that looked like electric worms wiggling through the air where the chair had just been. "That's what we call 'collapsing back to wave potential'. As long as you look at something it stays exactly as you expect, but the minute you look away and pay attention to something else, it stops being what it was!"

"Really?" asked Aiden, who had been trying to make the chair reappear again by looking intently at the wiggly lines. "How come I can't make it become a chair again?"

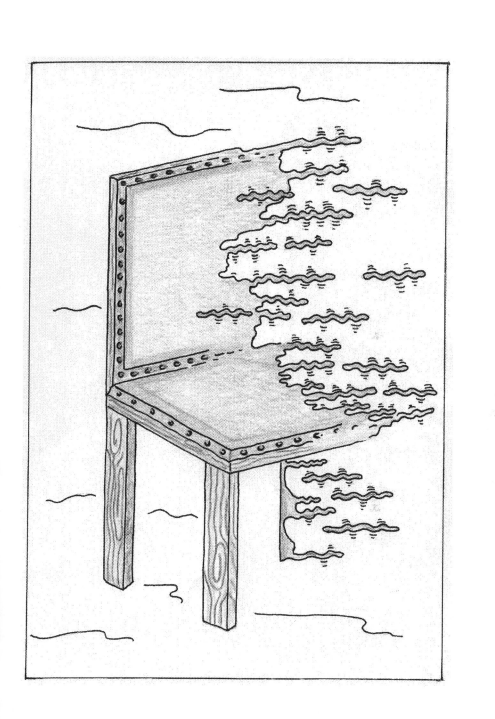

"Oh, you can, Aiden," Mr. Pierce replied. "I just kept it as waves to show you how it works. Now I'll put it back into space and time so it will behave normally." With that, the chair instantly appeared again. Aiden got up and knocked on the chair's seat with his knuckles just to make sure it was solid again.

"So the main point here is that nothing exists at all without our observing it in some way," Mr. Pierce continued. "Think about the moon. Whenever we look at it, we find it exactly where we expect it to be, moving along the path we have known it to take for most of our lives. We expect the moon to be there even when we are not looking at it, so when we look away the moon's possibility waves spread out a little – by a teeny bit, so teeny it isn't recognizable by most measuring equipment, but it does spread. When we look back at the moon the wave collapses in on itself and the particles reappear, making it the moon again."

Mr. Pierce looked around the room checking to see if his students understood his examples. It seemed as if everyone did, so he motioned for all to follow him as he said, "How about a ride? We can ride along and play with space and time, turning things from waves to particles and back to waves of potential."

All the students jumped to their feet and Chucky followed shyly as they summoned the horses grazing in the pasture. Tina chose Onyx again and pulled Chucky up behind her. He had been progressing nicely in his riding skills but Tina thought he would be happier riding with her in this new place.

Chucky sat quietly behind Tina and watched as she directed her attention towards a row of trees alongside the path they were riding on. She raised her hand and pointed her finger, waving as if to clear the trees away with a magic wand. Tina made them dissolve into waves of possibility as she turned her head to focus back to the path in front of her and then caused them to regain their particle state solidifying back into trees.

"Try this, Chucky. It's really fun!" cried Tina, flushed with excitement.

Chucky raised his hand and directed it towards the surface of a river off in the distance. A boat appeared to take shape slowly, becoming denser and gently bobbing where he had intended it to be.

"There, Tina! Look at my boat! I'd like to have one just like that one day," Chucky said, admiring his work. He had always wanted a sailboat. When he was younger his father used to take him sailing on his grandfather's little wooden sailboat. The boat he just made looked exactly like his grandfather's had.

"It's a nice boat. I'd love to sail on it, too! I wish we could create things as fast as this back in our world," Tina smiled. "We could have anything we wanted, couldn't we? Marguerite says we can, but it just takes longer there than it does here." Tina remembered how she had been annoyed at Marly once and had imagined her with a mustache, then thought it was better that things didn't take shape immediately in her world.

"Wait for me!" said Heather, who was riding at a fast trot to catch up to the group. She hadn't been at the open school with the rest of the class earlier. "Sorry I'm late today. I had to go with my mother and little brother to his creative class. What have I missed?"

"We are collapsing wave potentials into particles," Ben said, trying to sound very clever.

"Oh! I know what you mean. That's when we make things disappear and reappear," Heather said quickly.

"Well, yes, that is what it appears to be anyway," replied Mr. Pierce.

Not giving further chance for discussion on the matter, Heather rode right up next to Tina and Chucky. She interrupted and, in her attempt to get closer to Chucky, changed the subject. "So, Chucky, you decided to come to our world. At last! I've been waiting for you to come. It gets boring around here with the same old faces. So what have you been doing? Where have you been? Have you gotten a horse yet? Is Tina your girlfriend?"

"Oh, Heather! Leave him alone!" Jiankara interrupted before Heather had a chance to embarrass Chucky any further.

Chucky was blushing but managed to reply while ignoring the last question. "I have been riding Tina's mother's horse, Toby, for now. I'll get a horse of my own soon, I think. I haven't found the right one yet."

"I know the one waiting for you to find him. I can hear him now. He is saying that you will hear him speak to you when you get closer to him… He says you don't have the power yet to hear from animals at a big distance… He says he is coming from another part of the country," Heather reported.

"You can hear animals, too?" Chucky asked.

"Well, sure! We all can, here in this world anyway," Heather answered. "We think it is a little strange that in your world only a few people can hear from animals."

Mr. Pierce interrupted at this point. "Heather, you know how it is. Things operate differently in different worlds. Tina and Chucky are involved in a world where there are many things left to be discovered. That is the fun of it there. It's not 'strange', just 'different'."

"Yes. I know, Mr. Pierce. I didn't mean to make it sound like our world was better, or anything. It's just different," Heather replied. Mr. Pierce smiled and picked up the pace a little, the others following at a gentle trot.

The children rode along in silence for quite a while, enjoying the sunshine and the game of creating and collapsing all kinds of different objects that could be found in both of their worlds. The whole group had successfully made a new environment of green fields with lush vegetation, then let it dissolve away. They returned to the open school building and let the horses wander off to graze again.

"I think we had better be getting back to our world," Tina said, thinking about her classmates frozen in time. She looked across the pasture where she thought they might rejoin the Cosmic Lattice.

"Yes, I suppose you should. Please come back to visit us again soon. It was nice of you to come, too, Chucky," Mr. Pierce agreed, extending his hand to shake Chucky's.

"Thank you. I would like to come back again, Mr. Pierce," Chucky said, and shook his hand.

They headed off across the pasture and when they felt the air thicken in front of them they held hands and stepped through the imaginary doorway. This time they reappeared directly in their classroom without traveling the Cosmic Lattice.

"That was quick. I think I like going along the Lattice better though, don't you?" Tina asked Chucky.

"Yeah, it makes it easier to come back here," Chucky answered, taking note of everybody in exactly the same position they left them in hours earlier. To them it seemed hours had past, anyway, but here in their world time had stopped. They no sooner took their seats when the class resumed. Tina and Chucky glanced at each other and smiled, trying to suppress a giggle.

Chapter 2

Tina rode around lazily on Dancer's back through the big pasture where her horse spent the summer and early autumn days. She hadn't bothered to saddle Dancer, preferring instead to ride around bareback. She stretched herself over Dancer's back, resting her head on the horse's rump, bringing her bare feet up to rest on either side of the withers. She moved her feet in small circles around the withers, massaging the horse, then allowed the root of the mane to slip between her toes. Tina imagined if she were a monkey she would probably ride a horse with her feet as much as her hands.

The sunshine felt comforting on her face, and Tina closed her eyes to rest for a moment. She was tired from a long day at school and her trip to the 'other world' school as well. She thought about how wonderful her experiences were and how much she learned, whenever she went there. She thought about Chucky and how amazed he had been by the knowledge presented, and that he had not been nervous there about learning something new once he got used to the place. She also marveled at how quickly Chucky was able to focus his mind and create the wonderful sailboat. She wondered if Polly would be able to do likewise. Imagining that Polly could, Tina hoped to have a chance to travel along the Cosmic Lattice with her soon.

Just then Polly came strolling across the pasture, waving enthusiastically and called out, "Hi, Tina!"

Tina sat up and waved back, waiting until Polly had reached her before replying. "Hi, Polly. What have you been doing this afternoon?"

"I've just been at the barn talking to some of the other boarders and I found out there is a trick trainer coming to do a show right here in our town. He's famous, you know?" Polly chattered.

"Really? What's his name?" Tina asked.

"I don't know, but he *is* famous," Polly answered, sounding a little bit hurt thinking Tina hadn't believed her.

"Tell me about him, Polly," Tina added quickly, wondering if she had hurt Polly's feelings.

"Well, he goes all around the country talking to people about teaching their horses to do tricks. He shows you how to do some cool, easy things but he does crazy, tricky stuff, too!" Polly continued.

"Like what kind of stuff?" Tina prompted.

"Like he jumps his horses through flaming hoops! And he jumps off the back of them when they are galloping! Is that crazy?" Polly answered excitedly.

"That *is* crazy," Tina agreed, nodding her head. "Do we need tickets to go see him?"

"I should think so. We can ask back at the barn. You look lazy, Tina," Polly added, changing the subject.

"I'm tired. Remember I told you about the place I go to and about the kids at the 'other world'? I went there for hours during social studies today," Tina answered, yawning loudly.

"Did time stop for you again?" Polly asked, and Tina nodded.

"I can't imagine time stopping. What am I doing when you stop time?" Polly asked, becoming a little worried she was missing out on something important.

"I don't know. Maybe you just stop like everybody else," Tina answered, considering for the first time what must be actually happening to others when time stopped. She knew everyone seemed to freeze but she had never actually thought before what must be going on in their minds when it happened. She thought since they never seemed to remember anything that their minds must just freeze, too.

"Can I go with you next time, Tina?" Polly begged.

Tina considered for a minute and replied, "You would love it there, Polly! I want you to come with me. You and Chucky will get so used to it maybe you can even go without me if you like. Everybody is so nice there!"

"Let's go tomorrow!" Polly exclaimed, almost jumping with excitement at the thought of the journey. "We can go during lunchtime when we are all together. What do you have to do to stop time?"

"I don't know exactly. I guess I just thought about it and time stopped. I don't think I had to do anything. Let's go during lunch. I don't know what they will be learning tomorrow but I know it will be fun! It always is!" Tina answered, also getting excited about the idea of returning. The 'other world' had become her favorite place in which to spend time.

The girls left Dancer in her pasture and made their way back to the barn. There were very few horses at the barn area because most were out in farther pastures or on trails with their owners. Toby, the horse Chucky had been riding lately, was in his stall waiting for the ferrier to build him a new shoe since he had thrown the original one somewhere out in the pasture. Tina said "good-bye" to Polly who had to leave, and stepped into the stall to groom Toby while he waited.

"You are looking very good, Mr. Toby," Tina cooed as she ran the soft curry over his back. His golden coat glistened in the sunlight coming in through the little window in his stall. It was very warm in the barn, so Tina plugged in a box fan which was secured high above pointing down towards the stall, and felt the relief as the air moved around gently.

"That's better," she said, and continued to brush the Palomino lazily who now let his head drop slightly and drifted off to sleep. Tina quietly left the stall and sensed a feeling of gratitude coming from Toby for the attention she had just given him. She had been getting better at sensing what horses were thinking and feeling since she had been spending time with Chucky but she wished she could actually hear words from them like he could.

Tina strolled lazily back to her house, greeting Sheppi as he came running around the corner at full throttle. The dog was always a bundle of energy waiting to pounce and jump with excitement. Tina loved his enthusiasm for everything but especially she loved the way he was always so happy to see her.

She sat down on the grass and scratched Sheppi vigorously on the chest as he happily rolled over onto his back. Chucky had told her that Sheppi was always happy - at least that's what Sheppi told him, anyway. She believed it. As she sat there with Sheppi, she thought about Marly and wondered if she were ever happy. Marly certainly didn't seem so. She wondered whether Marly would want to travel with her sometime to the 'other world' or if she would be afraid. Tina thought that people who were generally unhappy seemed to be afraid of things, too.

"Do you know why that is, Tina?" Marguerite asked, taking shape next to Tina on the grass.

"No! I don't," Tina replied, quite surprised by Marguerite's voice.

"So sorry, Tina, I didn't mean to startle you," Marguerite apologized.

"That's okay, Marguerite," Tina reassured the angel. "I am used to your appearing all of a sudden!"

Marguerite smiled broadly and continued. "The reason people who are unhappy are afraid is because they have forgotten who they are. They have paid too much attention to things that make them feel less than they are – less wizard-like. They pay attention to scolding from others who think it's important to cut others 'down to size'. Shame, isn't it?"

"Yeah, I think so," Tina agreed.

"So when people forget who they truly are they feel like life controls them instead of the other way around. They think they are a teeny boat being tossed around in a scary sea of life instead of the captain of their powerful ship!" Marguerite explained.

"But why do people try to make others feel small?" Tina asked.

"They are not trying to be mean, exactly. They themselves have been made to feel small by others because people usually repeat what they have learned, even if it's not very helpful. They think they are making someone look at life realistically. It's as if they believe that seeing oneself as a powerful being instead of a small, leaky boat is unrealistic. Funny thing is, though, that's the 'unreal' thing! On top of that they don't understand that they are making their own reality anyway!" Marguerite explained further.

"Making their own reality?" Tina repeated.

"Yes. Tomorrow when you go to the 'other world' school you will find them involved in an interesting lesson about one very important law of the universe which will explain this. It will be a good time for Polly to join you there. You know how sometimes she thinks the world is picking on her. She might just gain some understanding about how she plays a part in that," Marguerite continued.

"Yes, she does. She always says that life isn't fair. I don't believe that," Tina stated.

"No, you don't, do you? More and more you understand that life is just something to experience, neither fair nor unfair. It's just what you decide it will be," Marguerite said.

"Marguerite, today was the first time I went to the 'other world' without you, but somehow I felt that I could do it. Were you there with me?" Tina asked.

"I am always with you but you don't need me to accompany you there because you have others to go with you now. You know how to come and go over the Lattice or just step through to the 'other world', as you call it," Marguerite said encouragingly.

"I like going over the Lattice best, though," Tina explained.

"You can go over it whenever you choose. It is a lovely thing to see, certainly," Marguerite agreed. "I must go now, Tina. Have fun tomorrow." With that, the angel vanished as quickly as she had appeared.

"Good bye, Marguerite," Tina said, after her angel had gone.

The next day Tina was a clock-watcher all morning, barely able to wait until lunchtime. She and Chucky met up with Polly in the lunchroom and quickly ate the soggy pasta with cheese provided as the school lunch and sat whispering about the adventure on which they were about to embark.

"What are you talking about?" Marly interrupted.

"Nothing! Bug out, Marly!" Chucky said, grumpily.

"I wasn't talking to you, dummy!" Marly shot back.

"We are just talking, Marly. Nothing special," Tina interjected, not wanting to explain just then. Now wasn't the time to tell Marly about the 'other world'. She knew there would be an opportunity sometime in the future. "Do you want to come and have lunch with us?"

"No. I am going out to talk to some other people. If I want to get elected as Class President I have to keep campaigning. I have to get someone other than Tina to vote for me!" answered Marly.

"I would vote for you if I were in your class, Marly," Polly said, kindly.

"Thanks, Polly. Of course you would! Who else would you vote for? That frog, Bruce, who thinks he can beat me in the election! I should think not!" said Marly in a typically ungracious tone. "See you later, Tina… and losers…" With that Marly swung her tray around and marched off.

"Why did you even invite her to sit with us, Tina? She is such a jerk!" Chucky said, irritated.

"Oh, don't worry about her. Remember I told you always to do what she doesn't expect? That's the way to get her to be nice," answered Tina.

"It didn't work for me," Polly said. "I tried to be nice and she just answered back meanly, as usual."

"Keep doing it, Polly. I promise it will work. Wait and see. If you answer her back meanly she will keep being mean. She did say 'thanks' after all. That was a start!" Tina added brightly.

"Yeah, I guess so. Can we go to the 'other world' now?" Polly asked, hopefully.

Tina thought it was a perfect time to go and with just that thought, with no other effort, all at once the people surrounding them were frozen in time.

"Cool!" exclaimed Polly. "So this is what happens when you stop time." She hopped up and ran around the cafeteria, looking closely at the children around her in amazement, just as Chucky had the day before.

"Come on, you guys. Let's go out and find the Lattice," Tina urged, moving towards the door to the school yard.

When they were all walking close together at the edge of the fence they felt the air thicken and Chucky was first to take hold of their hands. "Right, here it is. Let's step through," he said.

"Here *what* is?" Polly asked, looking around, not noticing the change that had taken place. Chucky pulled her slightly forward and the three of them pushed through the 'doorway' to the Lattice. "Huh?" she asked in surprise.

"This is it, Polly! This is the Cosmic Lattice. Isn't it beautiful?" Tina asked, brightly.

"It's… well, it's… amazing," Polly added, taken aback by the wonderful sight in front of them. "What are these things?" she asked, pointing to the illuminated, colorful globes surrounding them like stars.

"I don't know," Tina answered. "They are always here floating around. We'll ask Marguerite next time we see her. Do you hear the humming?"

"Yeah! What is that? It sounds like singing," Polly remarked.

"It does. I love it here. Let's move on, though," Tina urged.

They floated along the Lattice until they felt the thickening again and slipped through to the pasture by the 'other world' school once again. This time they were greeted by the entire herd of magic horses and the animals were glowing, welcoming the children with a feeling of excitement and anticipation.

"These are the horses we ride when we are here sometimes. See how they glow? When I brought Dancer with me here she even glowed!" Tina explained.

"They are beautiful," Polly said, admiring them.

"They are saying they would like us to hurry along because the kids are about to start their lesson… and we are invited to listen in," Chucky reported, listening to the horses.

"Hello, everyone! This is Polly, and you all remember, Chucky," Tina said cheerfully when they arrived at the open classroom.

Everyone greeted the newcomers excitedly and Mr. Pierce motioned them to a spare bale to join in the lesson. "So, friends, today we will speak about the Law of Attraction and creating your world exactly the way you intend it to be. We all remember what everything in the universe is made of, right?" he began.

"Yes, I do!" Seth called out. "Everything is made up of energy, always moving around to change forms but still just energy."

"That's right, Seth. It's all just energy," Mr. Pierce confirmed. "Thoughts are energy, too. They are the most important way we can control our lives. When we have a thought it carries a particular vibration out into the universe, making a statement about the way we see something. Let's say

17

we decide something is the color 'red'. We expect something to be 'red', the wave potential collapses into the particle of 'red' and we recognize it as 'red'. We have a thought that the thing is 'red' and it cements itself as 'red' within the universe. The only thing that will change that is if we decide to see it differently. Let's say we have a thought about it now being 'purple' instead of 'red'. We looked at it and we thought it might look a bit more 'purple' than 'red' so we sent that thought out. This goes on with such speed from mind to universe that we can barely tell which comes first, the thought or the actual event - unless we slow time down. When we slow things down we see that it is indeed the thought that comes first that makes the thing appear the color we intend."

"That's like asking which comes first, the chicken or the egg?" Tina said, quietly, and smiled.

"You are right, Tina. It is!" Mr. Pierce confirmed. "So now that we know our thoughts create what appears in front of us, how important does it seem that we spend most of our thoughts on what we actually want to create?"

"I would say! It is very important!" Tina said. "If we spent our time thinking about everything we didn't want, we would keep on making it happen over and over again."

"That's exactly it, Tina. A thought is nothing more than energy vibrating at a specific speed. By having the same thought over and over again you are creating that which you are thinking, but there is more to it. Creating situations and things has a lot more to do with feeling than simply thinking. The more energy you put into a thought the deeper your feeling about it becomes, so the clearer the instructions are to the quanta – the particles – that make up our world. What you see in your world right now is a direct result of what you have been thinking, feeling and believing!"

"But our brains are so busy all of the time. We can't control what we are thinking," Chucky said shyly.

"I know what you mean, my friend. We all have busy minds. So it is lucky that in your world, things take a certain amount of time to take shape. That gives you the time to sort out how you feel while considering some of your thoughts. The thoughts come through as information coming from all around you and that is useful in deciding what you do and what you do not want. It's up to you to decide which thoughts you settle upon and how you feel about them."

"But that's not fair," Polly piped in, whining just a little. "What if everybody makes me feel sad? I can't help that and then I always have to feel sad."

"Polly, no one can *make* you feel anything. The feeling part is totally up to you! How you choose to feel about the words and actions of others is up to you. When somebody does something to you that you don't like and it makes you feel sad, that gives you an opportunity to decide if you want that feeling. If you don't, then you can think about what he or she did in a different way and change the way you feel about it. That will change the frequency of the energy so those situations will stop coming into your life," Mr. Pierce answered, kindly.

"Oh," Polly said shyly.

"Don't feel bad about it, Polly. By feeling bad things as well as good things we can decide how we truly want to feel and what we really want in life. It's great! Having choice is great!" Mr. Pierce encouraged.

"It sounds like an awful lot of work to worry about what you are thinking about all of the time, Mr. Pierce," Chucky interjected.

"It doesn't have to be difficult at all because a random thought doesn't matter that much. What you can do is every now and again, have a look at how you are feeling about something and then look closer at how you have been thinking about something. Let's say you are feeling like you are not very good at something. Let's take riding a horse for an example. Let's say you are feeling like you will never learn to ride as well as Tina. If you keep feeling that way, guess what will be? You will not ride as well as Tina. If instead you recognize you feel that way and then shift your thoughts, what you think about instead is that, with practice, you are getting better and better. Then you begin to feel more accomplished and hopeful. That will most certainly cause you to ride as well as Tina," Mr. Pierce answered.

Chucky looked at Tina and realized that is exactly how he had been thinking and feeling.

"Let me caution you though," Mr. Pierce added. "If you think about it all the time and keep looking for the benchmarks of your improvement, then you will begin to create some anxiety around it. What do you think that will cause?"

"That would cause a bad feeling," Polly answered.

"Exactly! And what might that do?" he asked.

"That might make you feel like you couldn't do it, again," Chucky answered quickly.

"That might be what happens. There is a fine line between anticipating something happily and openly and anticipating something with doubt and anxiety. Look at what you want, expect it to show up, keep that feeling, and focus on the result you want. Using our horseback riding example, you could just enjoy riding as often as you could, practicing what Tina does and, in time, without any need for anxiety, you would happily reach your goal!" Mr. Pierce said, smiling broadly. "Look at every situation as if you have already accomplished it, feeling grateful that whatever you want in life can be yours."

"I know, Mr. Pierce, let's show them the tuning forks," Aiden said suddenly, and ran across the open classroom to a box which rested on the floor near the riding tack.

"Good idea!" Mr. Pierce agreed.

Aiden came back holding two tuning forks and handed one to Chucky. "Here, Chucky, hold this up in the air like this and don't move," he said. Aiden held the tuning fork at arm's length and moved across the room. When he was across the room he flicked one of the prongs, causing the tuning fork to begin vibrating, making a steady humming noise. He then moved closer to where Chucky was holding the other tuning fork, causing Chucky's fork to begin vibrating, making the exact same humming noise as Aiden's.

"See how that happens, Chucky? One fork set the vibration and the other picked up and began emitting the exact same vibration. That is a good example of how 'like' vibrations – 'like' energies – are attracted. That vibration could be an example of a thought or even a wave potential collapsing into a particle, couldn't it?" Mr. Pierce asked. Chucky nodded.

"You see, similar thoughts are attracted together, similar vibration and energy are attracted together, and so similar particles of matter are attracted together, creating what we see. That goes for creating situations too, not just matter. Thoughts and feelings create situations," Mr. Pierce explained further. "All right, enough of that for now."

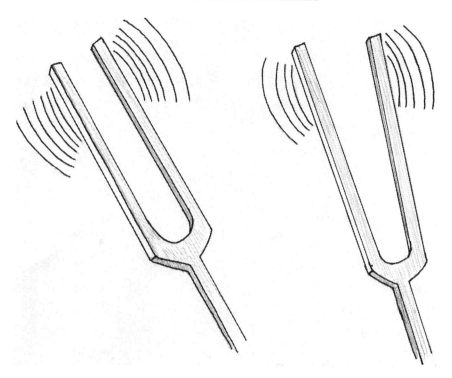

Polly looked at Tina, still a little confused about the whole idea of things simply appearing because somebody thought them into being. She thought a little longer about it and realized that she and Tina were like tuning forks vibrating at the same speed because they liked each other so much.

The horses had all gathered around to watch and there were a few nickers of interest from them when the tuning forks began their vibrations. Polly looked at the herd and decided which horse she would like to ride if she were given the chance. She spotted a little bay paint that looked like a sweet, friendly kind of horse and as she did the horse moved around the herd looking as if it were inviting her to ride.

"That horse wants you to come over to her," Chucky reported in a whisper.

"Oh, yeah, sure. How do you know that?" she asked teasingly.

"I just know," he responded, smiling. He hadn't told anyone other than Tina and Sequoia, the camp counselor, about his gift of hearing animals.

"Let's go for a ride with our friends, shall we?" asked Mr. Pierce, not waiting for an answer before he headed for the herd.

"This is cool," Polly said. "School with horses! What could be more fun?"

Chapter 3

They stood around the arena watching the horse warm up that the trick trainer was going to use for his demonstration. They had been lucky enough to get a preview of the trick training the famous Mr. Tarr was presenting to a huge audience at the big horse arena in town. One of the boarders at Tina's barn knew him well and had introduced him to some of the other boarders, including Tina, earlier that morning. He had some free time and had offered a little informal lesson to anyone at the barn.

"I'm glad we were here this morning, Tina, aren't you?" Polly asked.

"Yes, I am. It was a little bit of luck we were around to see this. I'm curious what kind of tricks he does," Tina answered.

They watched for some time in silence, admiring the horse trotting freely around the arena. "That horse looks a little like the horse you rode yesterday at the 'other world'. I love going there. Did you like it Polly?" Tina asked, thinking how they had ridden for hours after the quantum lesson.

"Now I see why you leave this world to go to their school. It's so much more fun there. Where is the 'other world', exactly?" Polly asked, looking at the sky for some sign of another planet.

"I don't know. The Cosmic Lattice seems to be a path to there but I can just think myself there, too. I think it's far away even though we can time travel there in an instant," Tina answered, considering her previous experiences with the Lattice.

"I think it's in another dimension altogether," Chucky stated, coming up behind them.

"Oh. Hi, Chucky," Tina said, surprised by his arrival. "What do you mean another dimension?"

"It seems too different to be in this universe. Do you think we can travel through dimensions?" Chucky prompted.

"I do!" Polly piped in. "I know angels do it all the time. My grandmother thinks they can. She told me!"

Tina remembered how Polly had told her the story of her grandmother and her angel and their experiences from a long time ago. Polly had even made a school project on angels during the winter. When Tina returned from camp she had admitted to Polly that she had an angel of her own. Polly had been jealous at first but Tina assured her that Polly also had angels around her and one day they would come forward to let her know they were there. "Marguerite told me that when we travel we can move through dimensions like moving through a layer cake of space and time. Like frosting, cake, frosting, cake. I like that idea!" Tina said.

"Me, too!" Polly added.

"When my mother was very sick during the winter I visited with her in another dimension… sort of," Tina said, remembering the night she thought her mother might die and Marguerite had arranged for Tina to meet her mother for a serious conversation about life.

"Look! They are about to start!" Chucky interrupted, noticing Mr. Tarr coming into the arena.

"Hello, everyone!" he called out to the crowd that had assembled around the arena. "My name is Thomas Tarr and I am here to give you an example of what I do with horses. The few things I will show you this morning every one of you can do with your horses no matter how trained they already are. This here is Jack. He is a 12-year old quarter horse who has been traveling with me for about a year. I have other horses more experienced than this one that I use for the fiery tricks, but Jack here is very calm and good for showing the basics."

Jack began a fast trot around the arena as if to show himself off to the crowd. "Okay, Jack. Come here please," Mr. Tarr instructed, and the horse responded instantly. "Jack was responding to my words but he was probably paying closer attention to my body. Did you notice how I made myself taller and planted my feet firmly? That little bit of movement gave him the idea even before the words came out of my mouth that I was asking him to come."

"That and the horse could read his intention before he even made his body do that," whispered Chucky.

"Do you think animals are faster than us at collapsing wave potential into particles?" asked Tina in a whisper.

"How do *I* know, Tina? Are you turning into a brainiac, too?" he responded teasingly in a whisper and smiled hugely.

"Nooo-wah," she whispered back, dragging out the 'o' and stressing the word by adding an extra forceful ending. "I'm just curious! That's all!"

Mr. Tarr continued to show them body language cues for simple things and then took a white stick which looked like a dressage crop from a bag at the edge of the arena.

"This is a cue stick which, when we first train a horse, we can use by touching different parts of the horse's body to tell him what we want him to do. Eventually the goal is not to use a cue stick at all, but have the horse read your body language entirely. I am going to show you how each step is done," Mr. Tarr continued, moving closer to the horse that had become bored and wandered off to sniff at the arena sand a few feet away.

The trainer gave lengthy and careful instruction, showing steps to make the horse bow, lie down and sit up all involving tapping the cue stick on legs, back, and rump to indicate the part the horse was to engage to follow the direction. He also used his body to cue the horse by bowing low, standing upright, and moving around the horse, stationing himself in different places. Everyone enjoyed the demonstration immensely and when it was over, several people went directly to their horses and attempted to copy what the trainer had just taught them.

Polly followed Mr. Tarr around, asking a stream of questions, while Chucky and Tina wandered off to find Dancer and Toby.

"What do you think about that, Chucky? Wouldn't it be easier to teach your horse tricks if you could just tell them what you want and they could ask you questions if they didn't understand what you were telling them?" Tina asked honestly.

"I thought he was pretty good for someone who can't hear from horses. His horse was very patient with him because the whole time the horse was having a conversation with another horse in that pasture over there and Mr. Tarr kept interrupting him! He was only paying a little attention to what the man was saying. He was sensing his body language more than paying attention to the words or the cue stick," Chucky answered, knowingly.

"It's funny, isn't it, when you know what's really going on?" Tina added cheerfully.

"Polly sure thought he was great. Too bad Marly wasn't around this morning. It would have been funny to see her pretending she could already do all of it. She would have been out there, taking the cue stick out of the guy's hand and showing him how to make the horse vote for her for Class President!" Chucky said, barely able to get the words out before laughing loudly at the thought.

Tina giggled and Polly caught up with them. "What are you laughing at?" she asked.

"We were just joking about Marly's way of getting Class President votes. Never mind. What did Mr. Tarr say to you?" Tina asked.

"He was telling me about a horse a friend of his has. The horse used to be a race horse and he even travelled with Mr. Tarr doing tricks for a little while, but he gave him to his friend last year. Anyway, the horse needs a home because his friend is sick and needs to go into the hospital," Polly answered excitedly. "I told him you were looking for a horse, Chucky. He said you should talk to him about it before he leaves!"

"Really? He's giving the horse away?" Chucky asked.

"Yes… to the right owner. Go talk to him!" Polly said quickly.

Chucky, Tina and Polly found Mr. Tarr and when it was decided that Chucky and 'Cruiser' were very likely a good match, arrangements were made for him to arrive the next day. As it turned out, the horse had been living very far away for the past year, but he had been staying at a farm nearby when the owner had gotten so ill recently.

The following morning Chucky, Polly and Tina assembled early at the barn to greet Cruiser as he arrived.

"I'll bet you are excited, Chucky! Did your parents say it was all right to get a horse now?" Polly asked.

"My dad had told me that as soon as I found the horse I wanted that I could get him and keep him here. My mom said that as long as I take care of everything about him, she didn't care which horse I got," Chucky answered.

"Oh, no, here comes Marly," Polly said, looking towards the road where Marly was just stepping out of her mother's car.

"What did she have to come for? Great way to ruin my day," mumbled Chucky.

"Hi, Marly," Tina said as Marly approached.

"Hi, Tina. Hi, losers. What's shakin'?" Marly asked, directing her question to Tina.

"Chucky's horse is arriving today," Tina answered, ignoring Marly's unfriendly greeting.

"You have a horse?" Marly asked, turning her attention to Chucky. "Since when?"

"Since none-of-your-business, Marly!" Chucky fired in response.

"Here they are now!" Tina said looking at the horse trailer pulling into the drive. "Oh, my goodness! It's Sequoia driving the trailer! Polly, that is the really nice horse lady from Camp Tarigo that I told you about."

"Sequoia!" Marly exclaimed, bursting towards the trailer as it pulled up.

Sequoia brought the trailer to a stop and pushed the door open to step out. "Hello, kids! Good to see you again," she said, smiling and hugging each one. "So this must be Polly. Tina told me about you, Polly. Maybe next summer you will be able to come to camp with these guys."

"Nice to meet you, Sequoia," Polly offered, politely.

"Is that my horse in there, Sequoia?" Chucky asked, peering into the side window of the trailer. His eyes met the tall horse's eyes and Cruiser let out a loud whinny, alerting every horse in the area to his arrival. "Whoa, buddy! You're a loud one!"

"That's right, Chucky. This is Cruiser, your new friend. When Mr. Tarr called me last night and told me who was taking Cruiser, I offered to be the one to bring him to you so I could see all of you guys," Sequoia said smiling. "He was staying at a farm near the camp. Let's bring him out."

They all stepped around the back of the trailer and stood back as Sequoia unlatched the back door and set the ramp down. He was a very tall, dark bay horse, a Standardbred, with a thick, black mane, and one white foot. Chucky stood back and watched as Tina stepped in beside the horse and led him out, being reluctant himself to step in.

"Here he is, Chucky. Here's Cruiser," Sequoia said, smiling at Chucky, knowing full well that Chucky had already begun communicating with the horse. She also knew of his gift of hearing from animals by the help he gave the vet in treating a horse at camp a few weeks earlier.

They all admired the handsome horse and Chucky took his lead to bring him to the nearest pasture where he could settle in by himself and whinny to the horses across the fence for the time being. They led him in and removed his halter and lead. They watched as he first trotted then cantered around the perimeter of the fenced pasture, tossing his head frequently and snorting.

"He's beautiful, Chucky," Tina said, feeling very happy for Chucky, who was beaming with pride and happiness.

"I'm so jealous!" Polly said, admiring the animal.

"I'm not!" Marly stated decisively and stuck her lower lip out in a pout. "It's just a horse. So what?"

"The so-what is, that it *is* a horse, Marly! Surely you must know by now that they make the best friends, other than people friends, that is. Look what a good friend Bucky has been to you," Tina said, referring to Marly's horse.

"Did you know, Marly, that horses have a special bond with people?" Sequoia asked gently. Marly shook her head, feeling a little silly for having said that about horses in front of Sequoia. "Let me explain a little bit about that to you. Horses act like mirrors for the people who ride them and care for them most. They mirror what is going on inside the person. They mirror the energy we put out by paying attention to our movements. If you are abrupt and jerk on the reins or dig their sides too much they become agitated and abrupt in return. If you are relaxed, then so are they."

"You can't fool a horse, can you, Sequoia?" Tina asked.

"No. That's what scares some people about horses. If a rider has been in conflict with people they tend to bring that with them as they ride and the horse and rider will also be in conflict. Also people treat horses as they are used to treating people. This can be a good thing or a bad thing and can work for or against a rider. The nice thing is if a person is brave enough to do things differently there will be no greater supporter than your horse!" Sequoia continued, hopefully.

"How do you mean?" Marly asked, warily.

"Well, if you are having a good day Bucky is probably doing everything he can to keep that going. He's probably more alert and happy, reading your body language and paying attention to your underlying emotions. They can read humans very well. So if you have been riding your horse in a bad mood every day and he isn't responding to you very well, then you decide to ride only when feeling positive and alert, the horse's behavior will change dramatically!" Sequoia explained.

"So what should we be thinking about when we are with our horse?" Polly asked.

"The best thing to do when you are with your horse is to give clear messages about what you want with your body and keep your thoughts on what you want to get from the horse. Try to stay focused in the present and not worry about what is coming in the future or what might have transpired in the past. If we are feeling fearful about something or if we are feeling smaller than we really are, horses will give us the opportunity to overcome that if we pay attention to how they are reacting to us. That gives us a chance to change our minds. It lets us choose our thoughts," Sequoia continued.

"That's what that law says: the Law of Attraction. You know, Tina, the one we learned about in the 'other world'. I mean…" Polly said absently, and then dropped her sentence realizing Marly and Sequoia might not have been supposed to know about it.

"What 'other world', Polly?" Marly asked insistently, turning her attention to Polly. "What are you talking about?"

"I mean… I," stammered Polly.

"C'mon, Polly, out with it! Where did you learn that? What law? You mean some kind of courtroom?" Marly insisted.

Tina gave a quick glance at Chucky who, in turn, gave a sharp look at Polly, telling her to be quiet with his glance.

"It's nothing, Marly. Just a place… You wouldn't be interested at all. It's… never mind," Polly answered trying to be evasive.

Marly turned towards Tina and asked, "Did you go somewhere without me? Somewhere friends are supposed to take each other? Is that why you took Polly? I thought I was your friend."

Tina was taken by surprise because although she had considered Marly sort of a friend, Tina never thought Marly considered herself anyone's friend.

"Marly, of course you are my friend. You just weren't exactly… around when we went. We'll go again," Tina said trying to find a way not to hurt her feelings.

"Well next time, I want to go to that courtroom, too then," Marly said, setting her lower lip into a pout again.

Chucky just smiled and Sequoia looked from child to child trying to figure out what they might be talking about.

"It's not exactly a courtroom and it's kind of hard to explain but, well… you'll see," Tina said.

Sequoia interrupted, sensing that whatever they were talking about it had apparently been resolved. "What I was going to say about changing your mind or, rather, choosing your mind, was that horses show us how to do that perfectly. They can switch very quickly from flight of fear to calm, reacting to their environment but not staying in a bad frame of mind for very long. Horses display pure joy often. Do humans?"

"Not too often," Tina answered. "Most people seem grumpy a good deal of the time."

"That's for sure," Chucky added, quietly.

"Well, most people are caught up into thinking they are not very good, or not very important, so they don't express joy very often. They see the world as a place where everything needs to be controlled, even their smiles and their laughter. They are afraid to be who they are. Horses aren't afraid to be who they are. They just *are*," Sequoia explained.

"So much less complicated to be a horse," Chucky said.

"I agree, but we are humans, and horses are with us to teach us to see our connection with everything, no matter who we think we are," Sequoia said.

"See, Marly, horses are so much more than they seem on the surface. Just like people, too, I think," Tina said, smiling at Marly.

"Yeah, I guess," Marly said, reluctantly.

Sequoia smiled and gave Marly a little hug before going back to secure the trailer ramp and door, preparing to leave. "Well, best of luck with Cruiser, Chucky," she said. "You know where I am if you need me. Come visit sometimes!" she directed at all three of them.

They said good-bye and returned to watch Cruiser get comfortable in his new environment.

Chapter 4

Chucky spent all morning watching Cruiser meander around the pasture sniffing, nibbling and rolling to acquaint himself with his new home. Cruiser spoke mostly in pictures to Chucky, showing the boy images, telepathically, of where he had come from and races he had won before he was retired. This was a little bit different than Chucky had experienced before with other horses that had used many words with a few pictures. Cruiser had been a harness racehorse, a horse they called a trotter because of the stride he used. Training had been difficult for the young gelding, starting when he was only five months old. He had run a real race for the first time when he was only a year old and ever since he had taken the business of racing very seriously. As a two year old he began to out-trot many of his horse friends, so he was moved to higher and higher level race tracks.

He continued to communicate with Chucky, showing how a man would attach a little buggy to him with long poles and leather straps so he could pull using his strong shoulders. The man would then climb in to the little sulky cart and place his feet wide and high into little stirrups attached to either side. He would hold the reins between his legs to control the direction Cruiser would take and use a whip to tap the horse on the rump when he needed more speed. Cruiser thought racing was thrilling! He loved to trot as fast as he could, never breaking his stride or faltering into a canter, just steadily moving his feet in perfect timing. Best of all he loved overtaking the other horses on a straightaway, then leaning closely into a turn, just missing the track fence by inches.

Sometimes racing could be dangerous, though. When Cruiser was only three years old, he needed surgery on his front leg because he had torn a tendon while showing off for a pretty little mare during training one morning. He admitted he should have been paying attention, but while racing around a curve he had turned his head completely so he could see the mare around his blinders, causing him to stumble. He fell forward, buckling his front legs awkwardly and the man spilled out of the sulky onto the track. Cruiser knew he was injured yet he was more worried about the man. He felt so foolish for becoming distracted while he was supposed to be concentrating. Cruiser tried to get up so he could check on the man, but he could not, as he was tangled in the reins and straps, and the pain in his leg made him buckle with every attempt.

Practice stopped and people came running onto the track to help. The man was shaken up, but was all right. He made his way over to Cruiser as soon as he got up, and began pulling the straps away to help the horse. The man had become very worried about Cruiser and shouted orders to the others to get the vet and help the horse up. Other than the pain in his leg, Cruiser felt fine and wished he could get the man to sense that. Later, the people helped Cruiser up and they brought him to a surgery center where he was treated like a king. He enjoyed his recovery time thoroughly, too, which lasted about six months and included wandering around a nice little pasture somewhere near Canada. A little girl came to give him carrots every day and when Cruiser had recovered enough she brought her sisters and brothers over for a ride. Cruiser loved to take the children for little strolls around the pasture on his back. By the time the six months were up, however, Cruiser was ready to get back to work. He was young and felt the calling to get back on the track and into the race.

Cruiser showed Chucky a picture with his mind of one very frightening thing that had happened at a race when he was four years old. It had been raining and the track was muddy, making it more difficult than usual to get into a winning stride. The man in the sulky was urging

Cruiser to go faster and when they got to a straightaway he continued to tap on Cruiser's rump. The horse looked straight ahead and saw that they were only a short distance from the next turn. Cruiser didn't know how he was going to pick up enough speed to overtake the horse and sulky in front, yet still be able to slow down enough to cut the turn and stay ahead. It was just then that he felt something wrench him sideways. The next thing he knew, he was sliding on his side in the mud, the sulky having flipped over, pulling him to the ground. He could see a tangled mass of sulkies, horses, leather straps, and men sliding into the railings with the horrible sounds of shouts, snorts, and crashes. One of his horse friends had to be put down after that wreck because of two broken legs. Cruiser was lucky to escape with a gash across his eyelid and a lot of sore muscles. He still carried the scar on his eye from the event, but he didn't dwell on that day much. No point in that when more of his race memories were pleasant than not!

Cruiser continued to race, bringing home trophies and big earnings for his owners until he was nearly ten years old, far older than most race horses. They loved Cruiser and were very grateful for all he had done for them, but as with most racehorse owners, they couldn't keep a horse around that was not earning money. They had known Mr. Tarr for some time and he had taught Cruiser some funny tricks over the years, so when it came time to retire, his owners gave Cruiser to Mr. Tarr. Cruiser traveled with Mr. Tarr for a while, doing tricks, but his old injuries made him feel really achy sometimes, and traveling long hours by trailer made him worse. Mr. Tarr then gave him back to the farm near Canada where Cruiser had spent all those months recovering when he had been only three years old. Unfortunately, very soon after he had arrived, his new owner had become ill. Cruiser had been moved to a farm near Tina and Chucky.

Tina came back to the pasture from the barn where she had spent the morning straightening up and helping the ferrier who had been shoeing a couple of difficult horses. Some horses just didn't want to be shod, but the experienced ferrier managed to do it and was grateful for Tina's help.

"What's Cruiser been telling you?" Tina asked Chucky

"He's been showing me all kinds of stuff about his life as a racehorse. Did you know he was a big winner? He told me how his people were proud of him and took very good care of him. He has had a good life but he has worked hard at racing. Look at his eye. He has a scar from a really big racing wreck," Chucky rattled on excitedly.

Cruiser came over to Tina and turned his head so she could see his injured eye. "Oh my, Cruiser, that's some scar you have there," she said, admiring the horse who seemed momentarily sad at the memory his battle wound invoked. Tina continued to fuss over him and rubbed his neck gently, noticing how broad his chest was for a Standardbred. She thought how he must have pulled a lot of miles to get such a broad chest.

"Chucky," Tina said. "I was thinking that, because Polly told Marly about the 'other world', maybe we should bring Marly next time."

"Oh no! She will forget about it if we don't mention it again. She's too mean. She wouldn't understand anything anyway. She'd probably just try to get votes from them and be obnoxious. It's all she knows how to do!" Chucky answered in horror.

"I'm not so sure about that. I think she might learn something and it just might make her nicer besides," Tina explained hopefully.

"Marly, nice?" Polly asked, joining Chucky and Tina at the pasture.

"Tina wants to bring Marly *for real*, to the 'other world'!" Chucky explained, still horrified at the suggestion.

"I'm sorry I told her, Tina. It just slipped. I didn't want to tell her..." Polly stammered.

"Oh, don't worry, Polly. I had thought about the possibility of bringing her anyway. She would like it, I think. Besides, I can't imagine she would ever forget about it," Tina answered.

"What do you think she will do there?" asked Chucky.

"I expect she will be her usual bossy self but it won't bother the kids in the 'other world'. They will find her funny. The Class President election is tomorrow anyway and we will wait until after that before we take her so she won't be campaigning!" Tina answered, smiling broadly.

"She will ruin everything!" Polly said, ignoring Tina's explanation. "She will drive them crazy and tell us never to go back there again and I only went once!"

"That's right, Tina. You don't see how mean she can be anymore because she has been nice to you lately. You probably have forgotten how she acts," Chucky said insistently.

Tina thought for a moment and looked back and forth at her friends. Maybe they were right, she thought. Maybe Marly *would* be as horrible as ever and then the kids in the 'other world' wouldn't want her to come back. "Wait a minute," she said. Why was she entertaining that thought at all? That's not what she believed. She knew Marly would need a lot of patience from her friends and she did consider herself Marly's friend.

"I haven't forgotten how she can be, but I also see something in her others don't, I guess. I want her to come with us," Tina stated emphatically. Chucky and Polly agreed reluctantly.

Cruiser stood dozing in the corner of the pasture, having settled in and having lost interest in the people conversation. Chucky approached him cautiously, not wanting to startle him awake but wanting to run his hands over the horse's shiny coat. Cruiser barely opened his eyelids when Chucky slipped his hand under the horse's mane and rubbed his fingertips in a swirling motion on Cruiser's neck.

"He likes this," Chucky said, satisfied that he could make his horse content.

Just then Cruiser surprised Chucky by folding one leg under and bending down into a graceful bow as if to say, 'thank you'.

~~~~~~

The next day the class elections were finally under way and by noon it had been decided that Marly would, once again, be Class President. Everybody knew that Marly would be the best person for the job, having proven herself the year before as the Class President who got an extra pizza meal a week for the whole school, not just the class.

"I won! I won!" Marly shouted while running down the hallway with a poster saying 'Be SMART - Vote for Marly!'

Chucky smiled, thinking how funny it would be if Tina made time stop right that second so Marly's bragging wouldn't be heard by anyone. He wasn't happy Marly would be coming along with them to the 'other world', but since Tina really wanted her to, he would try not to get into an argument with her.

After lunch, Tina thought it might be a good time to leave so she thought about the air thickening and where they would find the Cosmic Lattice across the yard. Time stopped and Chucky and Polly stepped up next to Marly who had been in the middle of talking to a happy voter who had been giving her a list of things she wanted the Class President to change about school.

"Well, I can't possibly do that!" Marly continued, not noticing at first that the girl had frozen in time while they had been talking. "Hello! Hello! Do you get that? Can you hear me?" Marly was puzzled.

"Come on, Marly. This is what happens when we leave for the 'other world'. Come with us," Tina said, reaching for Marly's sleeve and pulling her along.

Tina led a very surprised Marly to the yard where the thickening occurred, followed by Polly and Chucky who were still a little unhappy Marly was coming along.

They stepped through and Marly looked around nervously as the Cosmic Lattice took shape in front of them, stretching as far as they could see, glowing and humming ethereally.

"What's this? Why are we here?" Marly demanded.

"Relax, Marly, it's just how we get there. Enjoy it! It's beautiful," Polly said, encouragingly.

"I think it's weird here," Marly said. "It's spooky… not that I'm scared or anything!"

"No. Of course you're not, Marly. There's nothing to be afraid of here. We've all been here… well at least I have been here many times," Tina corrected herself quickly so Marly wouldn't think they had all been there so many times without her.

"I just don't understand it, that's all. What *is* this exactly?" Marly pressed.

"It's called the Cosmic Lattice. It's what is between here and there," Tina said, pointing way off into the distance where she expected they would come through to the 'other world'.

"Yeah, well, how do you know?" Marly asked curiously but impatiently.

"Helloooo," someone called out from some distance away and before long it became apparent that Marguerite was floating towards them, waving and smiling.

"Hi, Marguerite!" Tina exclaimed.

"Hi, all! This must be Polly - and this is Marly. How do you do?" the angel asked, first taking Polly's hand, then Marly's, and shaking it vigorously, knowing that if she didn't touch her Marly wouldn't believe what she was seeing.

"Nice to meet you, Marguerite," Polly said cheerfully.

"Uh… Hi…How did you know I am Marly?" she asked hesitatingly.

"I have seen you from a distance and Tina told me who you were, Marly. I am pleased to meet you at last," Marguerite said cheerfully.

"Nice… uh… to meet you, too," Marly said, again hesitating a little.

Marguerite smiled and looked at Chucky, "Hello, Chucky, good to see you again." Chucky nodded and smiled in agreement.

"So you were wondering about this Cosmic Lattice then?" the angel asked.

"Well, I was wondering, too, actually," Chucky said. "I know it is the way we get to the 'other world', but what is it exactly?"

"How'd you know we were talking about this? You weren't even here when we were…" Marly asked, searching the others' faces for confirmation that Marguerite really hadn't been there.

Tina figured that now was as good a time as any to tell Marly about the angel since, given they were travelling interdimensionally, nothing else would come as a huge surprise anyway.

"Marguerite is special. She's an… an angel, Marly," Tina offered.

Marly didn't say a word but looked up and down the angel, maybe looking for a halo or wings, but her gaze rested at Marguerite's feet where she saw her hovering above the Lattice. "Oh," she responded simply, not wanting to commit to expressing any emotion about what she was seeing. She wasn't quite sure what to think about it anyway.

Marguerite smiled at Marly, then put an arm around Chucky's shoulder. "Hear those buzzing and singing sounds? Those are thoughts coming and going along the Lattice. Each thought has its own tone range and color range when appearing in physical form. You see those globes of lighted colors floating around? Those are also thoughts with the added power of feeling. All those thoughts and all those feelings are what make things appear in your life. That is the Law of Attraction at work," Marguerite explained.

"The Cosmic Lattice is what connects all of us to each other and it is also where our thoughts and feelings are activated. It's sort of like the kitchen where life is prepared for you every time you request something," she continued. "It's a communication grid with thoughts and ideas coming, going and being shared across the universe. Quantum scientists, both in your world and the 'other world', refer to this grid as 'strings' in their 'super-string theory'. The thoughts and feelings that are activated on the grid cause the strings to vibrate at varying speeds and patterns, creating everything you experience."

"And it's really cool to travel on, too!" Polly added.

"That's right, it is. Since you are travelling to the place you call the 'other world' now, do you mind if I join you?" Marguerite asked.

"Yes, come with us, Marguerite!" Tina cried.

"What is the 'other world' then?" Marly asked.

"The 'other world' as you all call it, is another dimension. We angels like to call it a "place of higher consciousness". It is a place where people have decided to live a less difficult life and concentrate on different things than you do in your world. I promise the universe will unfold its secrets to you as you are ready to receive them. For now, why not just come along and experience what is revealed?" Marguerite suggested.

Chapter 5

They arrived at the pasture outside of the open classroom and as was fairly common by now, were met by the herd of horses. Polly went right up to the paint horse she had spent time with before and Chucky approached Onyx, apparently listening to something the horse had to say.

"Onyx says we should catch up with the rest of the kids across the other pasture over there because everyone is gathering under that big tree on the hill," Chucky reported, pointing in the direction of the big hill.

They made their way across the pastures on foot, Polly chattering away to Marguerite, Chucky in some apparent conversation with Onyx, and Marly staying as close to Tina as she could. Marly was uncharacteristically silent.

At last Tina said, "Marly, I know this seems odd to you because of the way we get here and all, but really, it is very familiar in some ways. The people seem normal but things happen here in a different way than where we come from. It's really fun though. You'll see."

Marly didn't answer but just smiled uncomfortably. When they had finally arrived at the tree everyone greeted each other and introductions were made to Marly.

"Wait a minute!" Heather said, knowingly. "You're the one Chucky doesn't like!"

"Heather! That's not nice. Maybe Chucky has changed his mind about her. You have, haven't you Chucky?" Jiankara asked, hopefully.

"Well, I… uh… I…" Chucky stammered. Although he really didn't like Marly, he felt uncomfortable telling the truth in front of Marly. He looked at Marguerite, hoping she would say something to get him off the hook.

"Chucky has had some difficult experiences with Marly, but it seems as if he is trying to give her a chance. Isn't that right, Chucky?" Marguerite asked.

"Uh… Yeah… She's here and… I am too," he answered, searching for something encouraging to say.

Marly couldn't keep her mouth shut any longer. "Be real, Chucky. You don't like me any more than I like you!"

Chucky didn't say anything, but took a seat next to Ben and waited for the conversation to change to another topic. Heather squeezed in next to Chucky and sat staring and smiling at him. This made Chucky squirm in discomfort and Ben just snickered a little.

"She likes you, Chuck. Lucky you!" he said sarcastically.

Chucky nudged him in the ribs and Ben flinched away from him, continuing to snicker.

Mr. Pierce cleared his throat to get everyone's attention. "Welcome, everyone. Today's experience involves getting you all to go deep within yourselves where you can have a conversation with all the parts of you."

"Huh?" Marly whispered in Tina's direction.

"Shhh, Marly, just listen. He'll explain," Tina whispered.

"Everyone get comfortable, relax, and close your eyes. We are going to take a walk through your imagination. Let's walk through a garden, along a pebbled path. Feel the stones under your shoes and hear them crunch as you wind your way through the garden. You are walking slowly and in the distance you hear water trickling into a stream. It's a little waterfall. You can tell by the sound," Mr. Pierce said in a quiet voice.

"Stop on the path for a moment. Now smell the air deeply. Breathe in and let it out slowly. Smell the fresh air. Breathe again. You decide to sit on a stone wall that is right next to the path for a few minutes and listen," he continued, then fell silent while the children listened to the sounds in their minds.

Tina was imagining the garden very easily but her thoughts kept drifting towards others in the group. She imagined Chucky probably wanted to doze off, Polly was bursting at the seams to start talking again, and Marly, no doubt, was ready to start demanding what this was all about. As if on cue Marly let out a huge sigh and shifted uncomfortably on the grass.

"Now, become aware of your whole body, starting at the tip of your toes. Feel them, wiggle them… now move up to your feet. Notice if they are aching or if they are relaxed. Notice your legs, starting from your ankles and moving up your thighs… feel them. Do they feel like they have been walking a great deal or just relaxing? Now up through your body…" Mr. Pierce said in a slow hypnotic voice. He continued instructing everyone to take notice of their bodies bit by bit, then asked them all to empty their heads of thoughts of anything except the feeling of their bodies.

Tina felt like falling asleep in the warm sunshine with the sound of Mr. Pierce's voice in the background.

"Now go deep inside to the middle of yourself. Feel the spot right in between your ribs, right in the middle, just below your heart. That's where you are - deep in there. That's the part of you that knows the answer to every question. When you get a little signal from that part of you that's you trying to talk to yourself! That is the *feeling* part of you talking to the *brain* part of you. It's what we call 'intuition' and that is one of the most important and perfect tools we have in our tool chest. We have minds that help us make our way through our lives but those brains are useless without the intuition! Brains can't do all of the work alone. They would confuse everything and never make a decision if it weren't for the intuition telling them what they need to pay attention to. Now take some time to listen to what that part of you is saying," Mr. Pierce continued, and then fell silent again.

After several minutes had passed, Mr. Pierce asked everyone to leave the garden of their minds gradually, and come back to the group. When everyone had opened their eyes and started feeling more awake he continued, "How did that feel to everyone? Anybody hear something interesting from deep inside of themselves?"

"Yeah! I heard my stomach growling," Aiden called out, causing the whole group, including Mr. Pierce, to laugh out loud.

"I'm sure you did, Aiden! But besides that, does anyone have anything to share?" he asked.

Jiankara was the first to speak up. "I was drifting through my mind garden and my feet weren't even touching the ground. I floated down the path to a huge tree where little pieces of paper were hanging off of each branch. They were notes but they weren't for me. They were meant for Marly and Polly."

Marly looked at Jiankara in amazement and Polly quickly asked, "What do you mean? They were for us? How do you know?"

"Well, my intuition told me," Jiankara answered simply.

"Jiankara is used to listening to herself, Polly. She was taught to pay attention to it when she was still a very little girl," Marguerite explained gently.

"Perhaps it would be helpful to Polly and Marly if you were to take them aside and explain everything you saw, Jiankara," Mr. Pierce suggested. "If they would like to, you could take them over there away from the group."

Polly looked at Marly, who still appeared quietly amazed, and nodded to answer Mr. Pierce.

"Marly, do you want to join them?" Mr. Pierce asked.

"Yeah, I guess so," Marly answered, curious about the messages, but mostly just feeling like she had to do what she was told. Marly didn't understand that in this world everyone did only what seemed most desirable.

Jiankara led Polly and Marly away from the group and sat in the shade of a large tree where the girls took a seat, cross legged, across from her, while the rest of the group continued their conversation about individual mind gardens.

"The tree I saw had little messages written on different colors of paper, hanging from the branches. Some had only a word on them and some had a whole paragraph. I could not read the messages because they weren't meant for me, but I knew some were for both of you."

"Did you hear someone say that to you?" Polly asked.

"No, not exactly. I didn't hear words really; I just had a feeling deep inside of me. I knew – I just 'knew'. That's how intuition works. Some people get a thought, followed by a little feeling in their stomach that sends them a signal letting them know their thought is true," Jiankara explained. "So when I thought the messages were for me I didn't get that feeling, but when I thought of you, Polly, and you, Marly, I got that little feeling and I instantly knew I was right."

"So how do *I* get that 'feeling'?" Marly asked, impatiently.

"You can learn it, Marly. Anyone can," Jiankara answered.

"Teach us how!" Polly interjected, excitedly.

"It will come with a lot of practice. Meanwhile, I can take you into the mind garden where you can see your messages. Do you want to do that?" Jiankara asked.

"I do!" Polly answered, quickly.

"Me, too," Marly added, a little reluctantly.

"Well, first thing you do is close your eyes and get comfortable again," Jiankara instructed, closing her eyes. "Imagine yourself walking down a narrow garden path winding through a green lawn. Notice all the little details you can. Someone has just mowed the grass so you can smell the freshly cut lawn… You keep walking, passing by tall, dark green hedges that smell of evergreen plants… Now you notice the big bushes of flowers around the path and you can smell them. Smells like perfume, one really strong, like your grandmother's perfume…"

Marly interrupted the description by sneezing loudly.

"Wow, Marly, you have a powerful imagination!" Jiankara joked. All three girls giggled a little bit and then Jiankara continued. "Now you can step off the path and walk through the grass. Feel how squishy it is, just like a thick carpet… Walk on it for a while until you see the big tree… I call this tree the "Grandmother Tree" because she is old and knows a lot. As you get closer, you can see her branches have hundreds of messages amongst the leaves. Some of the messages are for you, and you know exactly which ones they are…You pluck them off and take them with you…"

"You walk around the tree now… You see a door in her trunk just big enough to slip through to go inside… Go inside… Look around… You see hallways leading off from the main trunk room and you look down each one of them, deciding which one you want to go down… They don't go down, they go up… You choose one and wind up and up the trunk… Think about what you see… Every hallway has doors along it and you choose one to go through… Every door has a room behind it with helpful people or animals so it doesn't matter which one you choose…"

Jiankara paused a long time so Marly and Polly could use their imaginations to decide who they might meet in the rooms. "Ask them what the messages mean now… Pick one message and read it to the helper… What is it?" Jiankara prompted.

In her imagination, Polly entered a room where a dog was sitting on a red velvet pillow. He sat very still, wagging his tail in greeting, and Polly thought he seemed very wise by the expression on his face. She opened one of the messages she had plucked from the tree and it read, "School is difficult." Immediately, Polly thought she heard someone speaking to her, but no one other than the dog was in the imaginary room with her. She wondered if the dog were sending her the thoughts.

"Things are only as difficult as you think they are, Polly," the voice said. "If you focus on the things you do well and don't fight so hard against the things which don't come naturally to you, you will find life less difficult. Everyone has specific talents and those are the gifts you can use to make a wonderful life for yourself. Don't compete with anyone. Just do the best you can do for yourself. You are here to enjoy yourself."

Polly listened for more messages, but nothing more was said. The dog curled up on the pillow, closed his eyes, and settled in for a nap. She left the dog's room and wandered back through the hallway to the next door, which was partially open. There was no one in the room, but she stepped inside anyway and unfolded the second paper she had taken from the tree branches. This one read: "Everyone will think I am stupid". She waited, expecting an answer, but nothing happened. Eventually, two cats trotted into the room from under the thick curtains to the left of the window directly across from the door. They didn't seem to notice Polly standing in the middle of the room but she could hear their 'conversation' as if they were speaking out loud.

"I told you we would be late! She must have come and gone already, Brutus!"

"She'll come back later, Nesta. What was she worried about?"

"She worried that everyone would think she was stupid."

"That's silly," Nesta replied. "Humans are not stupid animals. Maybe they do stupid things sometimes but they are not *stupid*. I wonder why humans are so concerned about what others think of them anyway."

"I don't know. Very strange, indeed. A cat would never bother with such a silly concern. Cats know who they are regardless of what others might think. It is of no concern to us."

"Anyway she is certainly a very bright little human. She even sees much more than most humans do," replied Nesta.

"Do you think that is why she thinks she is stupid? I mean, you know how when people don't understand something that someone else can see, the unseeing person accuses the other of being 'different' or in this case, 'stupid'? What do you think?" Brutus asked.

"I think that's it exactly, Brutus. Humans are funny that way."

Polly listened carefully as she watched the cats wander around the room, sniffing and chatting. They left as abruptly as they had appeared, apparently without ever seeing Polly. She left the room, walked through the hallway and came to a door which also stood partially open.

She stepped into this last room and again found herself alone. She waited to see who or what would appear. Having remained alone for a few moments, she turned to leave, but then heard a voice in her head. At least she thought it was in her head because she couldn't see anyone speaking to her, animal or human.

"Open the last message, Polly," the voice said.

Polly did as she was directed and unfolded the note, reading the message out loud. "No one will like me."

The voice began again. "Not everyone in the world 'likes' everyone else, Polly. It is of no matter, just as the cats have told you. People who are of like-mind come together to form friendships. It is as if people speak a variety of different languages and those who speak yours become your friends while those who speak another become friends with others. The key to friendships is simply to be exactly who you are and friends will come to you. Everyone doesn't need to like you and you don't need to like everyone."

Polly found the voice comforting, like her grandmother's voice. She wished she were sitting in her grandmother's garden listening to her tell stories of when she was young. Polly decided she would tell her grandmother about the 'Grandmother Tree' as soon as she got home after school. "Thank you, um, *Tree Voice*," she said, not knowing what name to use. She felt the need to get back to the group since she imagined it was time to return to her own world.

"Leave your worries here, Polly. You needn't bring them with you. The Grandmother Tree takes care of them for you," the voice said, gently.

Polly placed all three messages on a table against the wall next to the door and turned to face the center of the room again. "Thank you, Tree Voice," she said, quietly.

"Come visit any time you have a worry, Polly. I am always waiting for you in the garden of your mind."

Polly turned and left the imaginary room making her way out of the tree and into the garden, following the path she had taken to get to the Grandmother Tree. She opened her eyes to find Jiankara leaning against the tree trunk and Marly, apparently fast asleep lying back on the grass with her hands behind her head.

Chapter 6

When they had awakened Marly, the girls rejoined the group which had been continuing their discussion on finding the different parts of themselves and were now taking a break, chatting quietly with each other in small groups. Polly and Marly joined Tina who was talking to Heather about the imaginary journey they had just taken.

"I like to go through the mind garden to get where I want to go. It's like going over the Cosmic Lattice, isn't it, Tina?" Heather asked.

"It is. You are right! Both of them can be seen if you close your eyes and imagine them. The only difference seems to be that you can see the Cosmic Lattice even with your eyes open," Tina observed.

"Yes, but did you know that you can do the same thing with your mind garden?"

"You can?" Tina asked incredulously.

"Well, you can but it takes a lot of practice and it is much easier in this world than in yours, Mr. Pierce has told me. Here we can make any scene appear in front of ourselves with some thought. That is what Mr. Pierce will show us how to do in the next lesson. We have tried it a little bit, but he is going to show us how to do it even more today," Heather said.

"That will be fun, won't it? What did you guys do with Jiankara?" Tina asked, turning to Polly.

"We went into the mind garden and found a tree. I went inside the tree and spoke to a dog, saw some cats and heard a voice from nowhere! It was so cool!" Polly reported enthusiastically.

"You went in the tree?" Tina asked.

"Yeah, it was amazing. There was a door and…"

"You saw a tree, and you went inside…" Marly stated, an edge of sarcasm in her tone. "Yeah, right."

"Really! I did, Marly! What did you see?" Polly asked, truly amazed that Marly seemed so disinterested in something so interesting.

"I saw nothing but the back of my eyelids as I dozed because there was nothing to see," Marly answered. She then turned and plopped down where she had been sitting before.

Tina didn't really believe that Marly was just disinterested. She thought that maybe Marly was acting that way because maybe she had not been able to let her imagination go and explore the mind garden as easily as Polly did. Before she had a chance to say anything further, Mr. Pierce interrupted.

"Okay, everyone, ready to get started again?" he asked.

"I'll tell you about it later," Polly whispered quickly to Tina.

The group reassembled on the grass, this time with Chucky taking a seat between Tina and Polly.

"The first thing to master before you can experience making up anything you want is to create what we call *mindfulness*," Mr. Pierce began. He paused a moment to look around at the children to see which ones looked confused and which ones apparently understood. He continued, "By recognizing exactly what is happening right now, you can forget what has happened in the past and what might come in the future and enjoy this moment, right here, right now, to the fullest. This moment is all that matters. Nothing else is important right now. In reality, you can only have this very moment you are in! It is the only thing that is real."

Ben squirmed in his seat and looked worried.

"What is it, Ben? What bothers you about that?" Mr. Pierce asked kindly.

"Yesterday, when I fell off of Onyx, I scraped my knee pretty badly. It sure feels real to me now even though it happened yesterday! Look at it.

See what I mean, it is still here, right now!" Ben explained, pointing to the big scabbed-over scrape on his knee.

"Yes, I see," Mr. Pierce said, looking carefully at Ben's knee. "Here's the interesting thing though, Ben. The pain from your injury is your body's way of communicating to you that you should try to avoid falling off of Onyx. Naturally you should learn from your mistake to keep from getting an even more serious injury. Now, try to use the memory to keep yourself grounded in the present."

"But why does the present moment seem so important to you?" persisted Ben.

"Living in this moment means you do not allow yourself to become distracted by the past or to become concerned about the future. Live in the present moment and you will free your mind to focus on healing your knee. This will make your knee heal! Focusing your mind is very powerful!" Mr. Pierce exclaimed.

Ben became all excited. "You mean, I can help myself heal just by focusing my mind on it?" Ben asked, amazed. He smiled as he marveled at the wonderful power he did not realize he had.

Mr. Pierce responded with enthusiasm. "Of course! Just focus your thoughts on anything you wish to achieve and you will achieve your goal," he stated. "This is what we call 'manifesting'. First though, let's continue with the 'mindfulness' part. Some of our friends need more experience focusing in the present."

Mr. Pierce continued. "Everybody get comfortable again. Close your eyes or, if you prefer, stare at an object that doesn't appear to move, like a tree."

Mr. Pierce paused, then said, "Now, breathe in through your mouths and let the air out through your nose. Do this a few times." Mr. Pierce led them by example breathing in and out slowly. "Good. Now keep breathing this way and let's do another 'body scan' at the same time."

Marly couldn't imagine what was coming next. So far this whole class had been the weirdest thing she had ever experienced. She thought there seemed to be an awful lot of imagining and she wondered when the actual class part would begin with books and note-taking.

"Does your body feel hot or cold? Mr. Pierce asked. "Let's find out if anything aches. Start with your toes, now your legs... knees... thighs... middle...back... arms... hands... neck...and your head." Between each suggestion, Mr. Pierce paused, giving his students a chance to feel. "Let's go back now, starting with your feet. Tighten, then relax. Go all the way up your body like we just did, tightening and relaxing each part." Again he paused to let the children do as he had suggested.

"Great! Now, when you feel like it, come back to focus here with the group again." Seeing that Ben was alert and staring at his grazed knee, he asked him to get the baskets which had appeared next to the big tree behind them and set them in the middle of the group. When everyone appeared ready Mr. Pierce continued. "Seth, why don't you give everyone a bag from the baskets? Thank you," he nodded, as Seth complied.

Seth handed each member of the group a little paper bag and Heather was the first to open hers, dumping the contents onto the ground. Fortunately, everything inside the bag was wrapped. It contained slices of fruit, chocolates and crackers. Tina carefully lined up the items, using her bag as a mat.

"Strawberries! My favorite!" Heather called out.

Mr. Pierce continued. "Let's take one of these strawberries and look at it. Notice every little thing about it... Now put it on the tip of your tongue... is it rough or smooth? Take a little bite... Is it sweet or a little sour? Juicy or not? What does it smell like?" Mr. Pierce prompted. The group repeated the same process for the other items and Mr. Pierce explained, "Doing this process with all of these things, or anything you are looking at for that matter, is focusing on the 'now'. It is being completely present in the moment and being only concerned about what is happening now. This is being *mindful*."

When everyone had finished the snacks and the remnants had been cleared away, the group came back to form a tight circle. Mr. Pierce continued. "I am holding in my hand an imaginary thing. I am going to describe it as I feel it, then I'm going to pass it to the next person to continue the description. Each person must turn the object into something else. For those who haven't played this game before, just watch. You'll get the idea when I pass it to Aiden. He has already played this game with me."

Marly thought this school seemed like an absurd place where no one could learn anything really useful. She wondered how anybody could even test you if all you did was feel things. After all, she thought, didn't everybody feel things differently?

"This object I have in my hand is round and has bumps all over it. I see it as pink and I feel it to be made of a rubber-like substance. It might be a ball but it feels hollow and I don't think it is filled with air enough to bounce. It feels too heavy for that. It smells like something sweet and if I touch it to my tongue it has a plastic taste. I don't think it is edible…" Mr. Pierce began the description. He passed the imaginary object on to Aiden.

"Well, I feel that it is round but not completely round. It is changing shape and now it seems like something oblong. It has a pointed part with a hole in it. Wait! The bumps are becoming prickly. It isn't smooth anymore. Now it is really prickly. Ouch! It's sharp! It has sharp spines all over it. It has a smooth part I can use to hold it. That part feels like a tail. I think it's a fish! Phew, it smells like a fish. I'm not going to taste it. Here, Tina, you take it," Aiden said, passing it on to Tina.

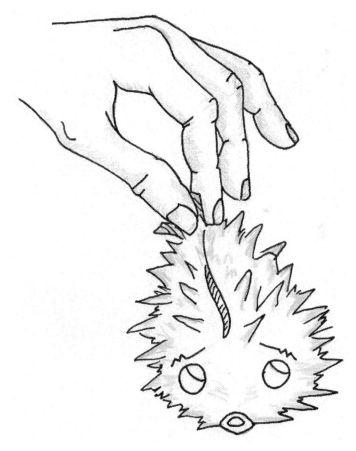

Tina took the imaginary object tentatively between her thumb and forefinger by what she imagined was the tail. She held it up as if to examine it and gently touched the tip of her finger onto the spines Aiden had just described. She didn't feel any. "This doesn't feel spiny anymore. I can press my fingers into it like it is something made of jelly. It's squishy! Wet, too. It's dripping... Eeew! Here, take it Chucky!"

Marly rolled her eyes and leaned back on the grass, removing herself slightly from the group. "This is not learning," she said to herself. "My mother would think this is a total waste of time. She says learning has to be serious, not fun." The game continued on this way until each member of the group had a chance to describe the ever-changing object into a new idea. When it reached Marly she took it reluctantly then passed it immediately on to Melanie who was sitting next to her. The children simply smiled and no one commented on Marly's decision not to participate. When the object returned to Mr. Pierce, he carefully placed it in front of him on the grass.

"Now let's move on to the *manifesting*. We've talked about this many times in a variety of different ways, but just a reminder: whether a thought or an object, everything is vibration, a movement of energy. We practiced manifesting things by collapsing wave potential into particles, so creating isn't new to you. You have practiced mindfulness which trains your mind to focus clearly and completely. The next step is to manifest that very thing you want," Mr. Pierce said, looking over the group and smiling.

"By focusing on how you want things to take shape you will be able to create that. Let's use Ben's knee as an example," Mr. Pierce said. "Ben, have you been focusing your mind on healing?" he asked.

"Yes, I have," answered Ben.

"Then let's have a look at your knee," Mr. Pierce asked.

Ben pulled up his jeans, and his eyes opened in surprise. "It's gone! The scrape is gone!" Ben cried in amazement. Everyone gathered around to examine the perfectly healed knee and Tina gasped in disbelief.

"Cool!" Chucky exclaimed.

"Well, how did you cause that?" Mr. Pierce asked.

"I... I don't know, exactly. I thought about it being just like it used to be and... I don't know what else," Ben answered.

"You simply expected it was. You felt happy and probably thankful that it was, so you manifested exactly that! Not so bad, huh?" Mr. Pierce pointed out cheerfully.

"I'd say!" Ben answered.

"But, Mr. Pierce, how come we can't make that happen so fast in our world?" Tina asked.

"You can, but it takes more practice there and not many people realize how to do it, or even believe they can. That's part of the problem. In your world, like here, if most everyone thinks a certain way, that is what becomes reality. Thoughts create reality. But, in your world, almost nobody believes in the power of thought. For those who do believe, it is almost like they need to swim against the tide of a strong ocean to create what they want. That makes it more difficult to do there," explained Mr. Pierce.

"I wish we lived here," Polly said sadly.

"You can come here anytime you want to, Polly. For now though, maybe you can be one of the people in your world who knows how to create her life and you can show others how to do it. What do you think about that?"

"I'd be afraid to," Polly answered quietly.

"You won't necessarily have to tell people in words. You could just be an example of how to do it. Do it for yourself and others can see what you do. Some will want to know how you do it and will ask you questions but mostly they will just watch. That won't be too uncomfortable, will it?" Mr. Pierce offered sympathetically.

"No, I guess not," Polly agreed, brightening a bit.

"We can do it together, Polly. You, Chucky, Marly and me. We can just know how to do it and others will want to know, too. We can be a different kind of teacher," Tina said excitedly.

Marly shot a glance at Tina, suddenly becoming annoyed that Tina had suggested she wanted to teach anyone anything that they had learned here in the other world. Truth was, Marly thought everything they did there was just play games. Stupid games, at that! Games that had no real use, were a waste of time and she was quite certain her parents would think this was a silly place to spend time. She was ready to leave, so she tried to get Tina's attention. She cleared her throat a couple of times, making it obvious she wanted something; then, when she had gotten Tina's attention, she used a hand signal to indicate they should leave.

Tina responded by getting up slowly and thanking Mr. Pierce and the others for the wonderful lessons of the day. Chucky, Polly and even Marly thanked Mr. Pierce. When they had said goodbye, they headed across the pasture back in the direction from which they had come. After waving goodbye to Marguerite at the entrance to the Lattice, they returned to their own world in silence, each lost in their own thoughts about their experiences at the 'other world' school.

~~~~~~

After school that afternoon Polly, Chucky and Tina met outside of Cruiser's pasture.

"How embarrassing that Marly is!" Polly stated, climbing onto the fence and swinging one leg over the top rail.

"She is so thick. She didn't learn anything at the 'other world' school. At least they didn't kick us out," Chucky said, grumpily.

"They wouldn't do that!" Tina said insistently. "How *Marly* is doesn't have anything to do with how *we* are. Besides, you never know what she might have been thinking the whole time. Maybe it is just so different there that she didn't know how to act. You guys know how important it is to her that she always feels at the top of everything. It is so different there she probably was completely lost!"

"Oh yeah, we know how Marly acts – when in doubt, be rude!" Chucky shot back and laughed out loud.

Polly giggled and Tina smiled in spite of herself. "Really though, she isn't so bad. Maybe she'll get it eventually. Maybe she can feel comfortable there some day," Tina said, hopefully.

Cruiser wandered over to the fence and nudged Polly's leg. Polly watched him without making any move and Chucky smiled.

"What does he want?" Polly asked, not really directing her question at anyone. She still didn't know that Chucky could hear animals' thoughts.

Cruiser slowly sniffed down her leg and gently took hold of her shoelace and tugged with his teeth, nearly pulling her off the fence before he let go.

"Hey! Quit it Cruiser!" Polly exclaimed.

Chucky and Tina laughed out loud and Polly couldn't resist a little giggle at the horse joke. "What a joker!" Polly said.

"He is saying that you should come and play with him because he has been bored since he arrived here… There are no horses nearby and he wants company," Chucky reported.

"What? How do you know he is thinking that?" Polly asked.

Tina looked at Chucky wondering if she should tell Polly but then decided to see what Chucky was going to say first. Chucky simply smiled and looked at Tina for encouragement. He was still so shy about telling anyone his secret talents.

"I just can, Polly. I can always hear what they are thinking," Chucky stated, simply.

"You can? How cool is that, Tina? Why didn't you guys ever tell me?" Polly asked.

"I didn't tell you because it was Chucky's secret. I don't tell secrets," Tina said.

"And I didn't tell you because I don't tell anyone," Chucky replied. Cruiser snorted loudly and stepped sideways, tossing his head in a further effort to invite the children to play. Chucky climbed up and hopped over the fence, landing directly in front of the horse. He suddenly bolted sideways and began running as fast as he could along the fence line. Cruiser took up the challenge and broke into a gallop, matching Chucky's stride. When the horse surpassed Chucky with little effort, Chucky quickly changed direction and ran hard the other way. Before long, Chucky ran out of breath and stopped, doubled over, holding his legs just above his knees and panting. He lifted his head to watch the horse's reaction and Cruiser reared up and struck at the air as if he were a horse boxer.

Polly and Tina laughed at the pair, then both girls popped over the fence to join in the game. Polly ran one direction, Tina in the other, and the horse galloped back and forth in an attempt to keep the game going. Chucky watched in amazement as the horse switched direction at top speed as gracefully as he had ever seen a horse do. For an older horse, Cruiser was amazing.

When the girls had tired of running they made their way back to the fence to join Chucky. "I think Cruiser really needs some friends, Chucky. Is it okay with you if I bring Dancer to this pasture so they can be friends?" Tina asked.

"Do you think he has adjusted to his new environment enough? He says he has but…" Chucky asked.

"Well if he says he has, let's give it a try. We can let Dancer stay in the pasture for a while, and then later we can put Toby in, too. I'll go get her," Tina offered, while popping over the fence. Within minutes she arrived back, leading Dancer who had perked up when catching sight of Cruiser. Chucky opened the gate for them, closing it quickly behind once they had entered. Tina unlatched Dancer's lead line and halter, allowing her the freedom to meet Cruiser. Tina and Chucky climbed onto the fence to sit next to Polly and watch the horse meeting.

Dancer stood quite still while Cruiser circled her. He began sniffing the grass, snorting, pretending not to pay attention to her. He never took his eyes off her, however. Dancer followed his movements with her eyes and waited for him to approach. After a few moments Cruiser crept closer, stopping a few feet directly in front of her. They both flared their nostrils, catching each other's scents, then Cruiser moved closer. Dancer raised her head up, nodding slightly and tensed her neck muscles as Cruiser rubbed his lips across her withers. She responded, doing the same movement in return, greeting each other as horses often do.

"He likes her," Chucky stated simply.

"I think she likes him, too!" Tina said, smiling.

They watched in silence for a long time as the horses got to know each other. They trotted around the fence line together, and then, while one grazed, the other tossed head and mane, reared slightly and bolted away. At one point, when Dancer seemed to be paying no attention at all to him, Cruiser lifted his head high, turned his neck on what appeared to be a very uncomfortable angle and pursed his lips out, showing his teeth.

"That is what a stallion or gelding almost always does when a mare comes into his pasture. Funny, isn't it?" Tina prompted.

Polly laughed and said, "It looks like he is sending her kisses!"

"Oh, come on, Polly! It's just a horse thing," Chucky said, embarrassed.

They continued to watch for several more minutes, then Tina asked, "Do you guys think it is possible to make really difficult things come true here in our world? I mean, like making school easier by focusing on it?"

"That's one of the things they told me in the tree, Tina!" Polly offered. "It was the dog who told me that if we focus on the things we do well and not get so upset about the things we don't do well, then school will be easier all the way around. He told me that we all have talents and we should pay attention to those talents, giving those things lots of attention. We just need to do the best we can."

"You heard from a dog?" Chucky asked. "I didn't know you could hear from animals!"

"I can't... normally, I guess. I heard from two cats in the tree, too. Here in our world I can't," Polly answered.

"Maybe you do, sort of, but you haven't realized you can yet. That's usually how it happens. First you think you can't, and then you think you might be able to. Then, before you know it, you hear random thoughts. Eventually you can tune in some of the time. Some people are so good at it they can hear almost everything that goes on in the animal world. I find that too confusing," Chucky explained.

"You know what else the dog told me?" Polly asked, then, not waiting for an answer, she continued. "He said that we are here to have fun!"

"Oh, sure! That is all ninnies like you are here for. Some of us are here for much more important things than that! Polly, it never stops amazing me how stupid you are!" Marly said, sharply. She had come up on them quietly and none of them had noticed her approaching.

"And what is so important about you, Marly?" Chucky asked, jumping to Polly's defense.

"I am important because I am here to work! Life isn't all games, you know. Things here in this world are not like that silly 'other world' you all run off to. That's not real!" Marly shot back.

"Not *real?*" Tina asked, becoming extremely annoyed at Marly's judgment. "You just don't understand, Marly. You haven't had the opportunity to understand the science of what *real* is!"

"Well, why don't you tell me since you know everything then?" Marly snapped.

"Here in our world it is the same as over there in the 'other world'. The only difference is the speed with which it happens. You saw Ben's knee, didn't you?" Tina asked.

"Yeah, so?"

"Well, that is the way things work. We can create anything – manifest anything. Just like Mr. Pierce said," Tina began.

"Nonsense!" Marly interrupted. "Everything in that place is nonsense! Just silly games and made up stuff!"

Chucky climbed down off the fence and beckoned Polly to follow him. "Come on. She's not worth talking to."

Polly followed and looked at Tina to see if she were going to leave Marly there, too.

"See you guys later. I am going to explain some of what we learned about how we create everything to Marly," Tina said. She was making a great effort not to be insulted by Marly's nasty comments. She understood that Marly was reacting this way just because she had always been told that life was supposed to be difficult and not any fun.

Polly followed Chucky back to the barn, leaving Tina to attempt to teach Marly some of the quantum physics and the Law of Attraction they had learned.

Chapter 7

Polly and Chucky swept the barn alleyway and tidied up the tack room before heading into the arena area to watch Mr. Tarr. He had returned to work with one of the boarders' horses. The woman who owned the horse had been using Mr. Tarr's methods of teaching her horse some tricks. She did some trick riding but wanted to teach the horse some tricks on his own so she could put together a little show of interesting horsemanship techniques with a lot of flair.

Chucky smiled as he heard the horse's thoughts. It seemed the horse thought he was doing exactly as he was told but Mr. Tarr didn't think so.

"Not like that, Horse. Like this," Mr. Tarr prompted, kindly. He touched the horse's front leg with his cue stick very gently so the horse would keep retreating from the pressure and fold his legs to lie down. When he had gotten the horse down, Mr. Tarr touched the horse on the shoulder, prompting him to sit up. "That's it! Good boy! Now stay right there. Stay sitting."

Chucky heard the horse thinking that a horse doesn't stay like that for more than a moment, on purpose at least. The horse thought how silly these things were that the man was asking him to do. He did sense how important it seemed to be to his owner, so he figured he would humor the man and do as he asked.

"That looks funny, doesn't it, Chucky?" Polly asked, smiling broadly.

"He looks like a huge dog. I think it looks awkward, but I guess it will look really good when they put it into the show. Where is she going to do the shows? Do you know?" Chucky asked.

"She is doing the first big horse show in Massachusetts, in the winter, then she is going to set up a trick riding school somewhere. I wouldn't have the guts to do that kind of riding, would you?"

"I'd have the guts but I don't want to get run over by a horse. The horse wouldn't mean to but they are big and sometimes they can't help themselves. They just move and if you were in the way, you would be toast!" Chucky said, honestly.

"Yeah, really flat toast!" Polly laughed.

Mr. Tarr made his way over to Chucky and Polly at the arena fence. "Good to see you, Chuck, Miss. How's it going with Cruiser? Have you ridden him yet?"

"Uh, no, Mr. Tarr, I was letting him get used to the place first," Chucky answered.

"That's good of you, Chuck. He's a great horse. He will treat you well. When you ride him just look out for his very pronounced trot! Remember he was a trotter so you will either want to post with him staying in his rhythm… which isn't easy… or just up until he smoothes out into a canter. It took me quite a while to get him to understand he could break out of his trot stride and actually move more smoothly at a canter. When a trotter is trained he is never encouraged to break that trot. It is what he does – he trots!" Mr. Tarr explained.

"Yeah, and fast, too!" Polly added quickly.

"That's right, young lady. Faster the better! Have you ever been to the Harness Races?" Mr. Tarr asked.

"No," Chucky answered.

"No, me either," Polly added.

"You should go sometime. It's very entertaining!" Mr. Tarr exclaimed.

"Do you think the horses like to race, Mr. Tarr?" Polly asked, thinking that maybe they did it because their people wanted them to, just like the horse learning how to sit in the arena in front of them.

"I think most of them do, but I am sure many don't. You know, sometimes I can hear them. Or at least I think I can. Sometimes they complain to each other. In fact, I'm sure of it. It's not that they use words, exactly… sometimes… well never mind," Mr. Tarr began and then let his voice trail off.

Chucky and Polly looked at each other knowingly. "You know what, Mr. Tarr?" Polly began, and Chucky shot her a quick glance, momentarily concerned that she would tell Mr. Tarr about his secret gift. Polly ignored him and continued. "I think lots of people hear what animals are thinking. They are just too shy to admit it."

"You might be right, Polly. Can you hear what they think?"

"Who me? No. Not me, but I know someone who can…" Polly said proudly.

Quickly Chucky interrupted again, worried that Polly wouldn't be able to help herself and tell. "Yeah… but, um… Mr. Tarr, do you ever hear what the horses that do tricks for you are thinking?"

"Oh, I don't know. Sometimes I think they are only half paying attention to me and half chatting noisily with their friends – just like a classroom full of kids!" he added, chuckling.

Chucky laughed because he knew that was exactly what was going on. He thought he must tell Tina about this. She would laugh, too. Mr. Tarr wished Chucky good luck and returned to the horse he was training. Chucky and Polly made their way back to join Tina, hoping Marly had learned a thing or two and was now long gone.

Tina was still sitting on the fence. Marly had gone and Marguerite had joined Tina. They were involved in a deep discussion when Chucky and Polly arrived.

"I'm just leaving now, kids," Marguerite said, smiling. "I'll see you all again. Remember, Tina, that is how we are all *one*," she said as she vanished.

"What did she mean by that, Tina?" Chucky asked.

"Marguerite was reminding me that every person you encounter and everything that happens to you creates an opportunity to learn something about yourself. I was telling her how I had tried to get Marly to listen as the universe spoke to her, but Marly just won't. She thinks I played a trick on her, that I'm trying to make her think she really travelled somewhere with us. She doesn't believe in the 'other world' even though she saw it for herself!"

"She must be stupid or something! And here I thought she was a brain!" Chucky added.

"She's not stupid. She is just afraid to learn a new way of thinking, a new way of experiencing. Marguerite reminded me that Marly is used to doing things exactly as she is told by her parents and her teachers. She only believes what they tell her is true. But, what she doesn't understand is that they don't know the lessons of the 'other world' because nobody ever told them. I was getting mad at her so I stopped talking and let her go away thinking anything she wanted. That's when Marguerite came and reminded me that we are all part of the same thing," Tina explained.

"You mean like we are all made of the same energy? Like a big soup?" Polly asked.

"Oh yeah, I get it! We are a good soup and then along comes Marly, the rotten egg that ruins it all!" Chucky added, laughing at his own joke.

Tina and Polly both giggled then Tina added, "No, not really. Maybe the soup can turn the rotten thing to good in the real world. We can put up with her the way she is, be who we want to be, then one day we may find her being a lot like us. That would be cool."

"Sure would. I won't hold my breath, though," Chucky said.

"It's still so hard to be nice to her when she is being so mean and stupid about things," Polly said.

Tina was quiet a moment while she thought, then continued. "I think that every nice thing we do for Marly and every time we act patiently towards her, it is really like giving a present to ourselves. Instead of feeling grumpy about her we can feel hopeful about her. I mean, if we are all the same thing anyway then whatever we do to her we are doing to ourselves. Right?"

"I guess so," Chucky said, after a long pause. He was trying to figure out if he could be that nice. It didn't feel like Marly was a part of him or that he was a part of her. He felt completely different and separate from her, simply because he didn't like her.

"Maybe at least that would make us feel better, even if we didn't think about it like we were doing something *nice* for her. She doesn't make me feel very *nice*," Polly added.

"You don't have to like her, but knowing that what we focus on makes for what we get in our lives, then I think it best to focus on what feels better, even with Marly," Tina said, wisely.

They sat in silence for quite a while watching the horses graze and swish the flies away with their long tails. Eventually Chucky broke the silence. "Do you think I should ride Cruiser today, Tina?"

"Sure, Chucky, maybe just a little. It will be the best way to get to know him and he is supposed to be really well trained, right?"

"I guess… we'll see," Chucky answered tentatively.

They led Cruiser to the barn where they tacked him up easily. The horse seemed quite happy to be readied for a ride and stood completely still even while Chucky cinched his girth tightly. They led him into the indoor arena and Chucky climbed into the saddle while Tina held the horse's reins. Chucky rode around the arena quietly, trying out Cruiser's different paces. He laughed out loud when the horse stepped up to a fast trot.

"That is the weirdest feeling!" he said. "You should try this, Tina. I feel like I'm going to bounce right off his back!"

"Just stay up until you can get him to smooth that out," Tina prompted quickly.

Chucky steadied himself into a half sitting position, squeezing his knees into the saddle to hold himself up like a jockey. He clicked his tongue, signaling Cruiser to speed up. "That's better," he said, settling back into the saddle as Cruiser loped around the arena. "He feels smooth like this."

Tina and Polly climbed up onto the rails, balancing themselves comfortably while they watched Chucky and Cruiser get to know each other. Marguerite appeared next to them, seated exactly as they were.

"They look good, don't they?" she offered cheerfully.

"They do!" Tina answered.

They watched while Chucky continued around a few more times, then settled Cruiser into a walk. The horse began following imaginary patterns in the sand of the arena floor.

Polly suddenly jumped off the rail fence, "Oh my! I have to go! I promised I would be home early for dinner so my mom and I could go shopping before the stores close. See you tomorrow!" Polly said. She waved and jogged off, not waiting for a reply.

The others waved after her and Chucky rode over to the fence where Tina and Marguerite were sitting. Cruiser seemed content to stand in front of them, letting his head drop slightly into a restful pose while they conversed.

"Chucky, I've been thinking there is something Marguerite would be much better explaining to you than I would. Remember how I told you sometimes we could see people in different times in different *dimensions*?" Tina asked.

"What? When are you talking about?"

"Well, I mean in the winter time. I told you, I met you as an older person. Remember?" Tina continued.

"Yes, I remember. I still don't see how," he answered.

"Maybe Marguerite can explain. I don't know if I get it either," Tina said, looking at Marguerite to continue.

"Chucky, when Tina was seeing you as a grownup she was seeing a 'potential' in your future. She saw you as an adult you might become. This is how it works, you see. There are any number of potentials for every person in the world. Each situation and circumstance creates another possibility," Marguerite explained.

"That is so complicated!" Tina exclaimed.

"Well, yes, but it doesn't matter which one takes place because every one of them actually does take place," she continued. "And to make things even more complicated, they are all occurring at the same time."

"Huh? How can that be happening? Only one thing happens at a time…" Chucky said.

"I know it seems that way to you here in your world. That's the way it is designed. But even here in your world scientists are discovering that time is not a constant measurable thing. It is not a thing that marches on, it is something you move through like walking through a room. This will come as a huge surprise to you but it is you who creates the thing you call *time* and it changes according to what you are creating. Have you ever noticed how time seems to drag along when you are waiting for something important to happen?"

"Yes! Or worse yet, when you're sitting in a boring class and time won't hurry up!" Tina exclaimed. "But I didn't think I had anything to do with that."

"Well you do… and you don't. It is more complicated than just being able to will time according to what you need it to do, at least on the level you are operating on. There are some who manage to manipulate it and some who have come close in the past to time travel. That's an exciting thing to play with," Marguerite said, smiling.

"I'd like to build a time machine!" Tina interrupted.

"So would I!" Chucky added.

"Could we do that?" Tina asked, looking at Marguerite.

"You could work on that. For now, though, you can get a lot of information from looking at the differences between this world and the 'other world', as you call it," Marguerite suggested.

"But I still don't get how we can be in two places at the same time like when I was old and young at the same time," Chucky prompted.

"As you experience what seems to you as moving between different dimensions you are actually moving between *realities*. In other words, each thing you are experiencing is real and happening in its own *time* but all at once. When you were coming into this dimension to see Tina you were bringing your *realities* together into one. You did this but not the *you* right here, the greater *you*. The *you* that has all of the perspective and can see all of the potentials and possibilities you are experiencing. That's your higher self," Marguerite continued to explain.

"That's like when I met my mother's higher self this winter. She could see different possibilities for herself all at one time and we talked about what she was going to do as the part of herself I knew as my mom. Is that right, Marguerite?" Tina interjected.

"Yes, that's right, Tina. So when you were Chucky as the boy and Chucky as the grownup you did a trick that most people don't get to do here. You travelled through a wormhole which is like a tunnel to another reality. You also travelled in time and just to make it really fun, you even came as another type of being," Marguerite explained.

"I what?" Chucky asked.

"You came to meet Tina as a cat, too."

"I don't remember that! How was I a cat, too?" Chucky asked, astonished.

"Just another reality! You managed to collapse them into one place and time," Marguerite explained further.

"Wow! That's really cool! Did you know the cat was me, Tina?" Chucky asked.

"Well, not at first, but then I saw the cat turn into a man and that was you in the future, or a potential future anyway. You'll be happy to know, Chucky, that you didn't do that future because we already changed things. We weren't friends in that future, but when we became friends at camp we made a new future!" Tina explained excitedly.

"That is incredibly cool. I wish I remembered any of it! I travelled through wormholes?" Chucky asked.

"Wormholes are where your past and present selves can come together and exchange information to create a future," Marguerite explained.

"So I was in a wormhole where I met my mom in her present, but not the one who was sick lying in her hospital bed… the one I thought was her… Boy, I'm confused!" Tina said, feeling muddled.

"That's it, more or less, though. Even though it seems to you that everything is happening in a past, then present, then future, it is all happening in the moment of now! The wonderful thing about now is that it's the only thing that is really real! You can think back on the past and project into the future but they are only happening in your imagination and not really in the present. That makes past and future unimportant compared to now. The only thing that you need concentrate on is right now. I've told you this before," Marguerite said. "Dogs always stay in the here and now."

"I remember that, but how can we make up a future if we don't think about it?" Tina asked.

"Oh, I don't mean that you shouldn't think about it. It's great to think about lots of different possibilities for your future. But if you spend all of your time imagining that, then you will certainly miss what is right in front of you. That's one of the lessons we can learn from dogs, remember?"

"Wait a minute," Chucky interrupted. "If all things and all possibilities are happening all at once, then where are these other realities actually happening?"

"They are taking place in parallel universes," Marguerite stated simply.

"Parallel universes?" Tina asked, trying to imagine what that could be.

"Did you think there was only one universe?" Marguerite asked.

"Well, yeah... kind of..." Tina answered hesitatingly.

"There are as many universes as there are possible futures. That would be an infinite number, wouldn't it?" Marguerite prompted.

"Yeah, I guess so. Wow!" Tina said, amazed.

"Wow!" Chucky stated in equal amazement.

"Wow, indeed. It makes life more interesting doesn't it? All those potentials and all those realities... What wonderful places these universes are!" Marguerite said, looking around and smiling.

Cruiser suddenly awakened from his dozing and snorted loudly, startling Chucky and almost unseating him from the saddle. "Cruiser says that he is hungry in *this* reality, so if I don't mind..." Chucky laughed.

"I will be going now. Good bye," Marguerite said, smiling and vanishing slowly.

"Good bye, Marguerite," Tina said, as she watched the angel disappear. She turned her attention towards Chucky and Cruiser. "I'll go get some grain while you untack Cruiser and put the saddle away."

Chucky and Tina finished with their horses and continued to discuss new ideas about parallel universes as they walked home.

"I have an idea, Chucky. Tomorrow, instead of visiting the 'other world', let's see if the Cosmic Lattice will bring us to a parallel universe," Tina suggested.

"Yeah! Okay! Do you think the Cosmic Lattice is really a wormhole?" Chucky asked, looking around to see if a wormhole would suddenly appear.

"I don't know... maybe," Tina pondered.

Chapter 8

The next morning the school day was crawling along in its own typically slow fashion. Tina's mind began to wander as she thought about what Marguerite had taught her about time, how slowly it seemed to pass! She wondered what might be happening in a parallel universe and if school were the same. She also began to wonder if the 'other world' were a parallel universe, about how she and the children there were able to move in and out of each other's universe. She began to get confused, and snapped back to the present. She looked around the classroom in her current universe. Everyone was still in the frozen-in-time state she sometimes created by simply letting her mind wander.

Chucky walked through the classroom door having just been out to deliver some papers to the main office for the teacher. "Oh! I see you have been thinking about the 'other world'. Shall we go?"

"Yes. Actually I was wondering about parallel universes. Let's see where the Cosmic Lattice takes us," Tina answered, moving towards the door.

They left the school building and crossed the yard as they always did to find the thickening air leading to the Lattice. This time they felt it before the usual place and stepped through, expecting the Lattice to appear as usual. It did not! This time it appeared as a thick swirling cloud around them, changing colors and thickness as it swirled. They couldn't see their way through the cloud enough to navigate the direction, yet somehow they knew they were moving through it. They looked at their feet to see if they were passing over a surface and occasionally caught a glimpse of the familiar Lattice below.

"This looks like a storm happening over the Lattice. I wonder if it is taking us to a different place," Tina observed.

"I'll bet it is," Chucky said, quietly.

Before long they arrived at what appeared to be the same school yard they had just left.

"Hey, look where we are!" Tina exclaimed, disappointed. "We're back where we started."

"Never mind. I guess this isn't the day we are travelling to the 'other world'. I wonder what happened?" Chucky asked, looking around.

They made their way back to the school building and entered the classroom they thought they had just left. They found the other students milling around, working on projects and talking quietly.

"Oh, there you are!" Marly said, running up to them, taking Tina by the hand and pulling her to her desk where a project lay waiting for a few more details to be added. "I have done the writing part, but knowing that Chucky is so good at art I thought you and he might want to finish the rest. I didn't want to steal the show! After all, we are a team!" she explained.

Chucky looked at Marly in amazement. Tina also had been looking at Marly, an expression of disbelief on her face.

Neither said a word, so Marly asked, "What? What did I say?"

"Uh… nothing… It's just that… nothing," Chucky stammered.

"Right, then! I will go write a little bit more and you guys can get started. Okay?" Marly smiled and walked away without waiting for an answer.

"What? Who… who is that? That's not Marly! She's never been that nice to anyone in her entire life! She must be ill or something!" Chucky said in a whisper, so no one other than Tina would hear.

Tina just shrugged and turned to the project in front of her. "I don't remember working on a project with Marly. In fact, I don't remember any of these projects…" she said, looking at the collection of brightly-colored posters on the wall. "Chucky, this isn't our classroom. Where are we?"

Chucky looked around the room recognizing everyone in it but not the details. The desks were situated differently. The displays of student work were different, too. "You are right. This is not our classroom," he whispered.

They continued to watch the other children in the room who looked exactly like the ones they had left, yet there was something different about them. They seemed cheerful and busily engaged in the projects they were working on instead of sitting in rows, staring at the teacher droning on in a monotone voice, as was happening in the classroom they had just left.

"What is going on?" Tina whispered back.

After a moment Chucky shrugged and said, "Let's just keep watching and we can look this project over to see what it needs. We might as well have some fun while we are here… in this other dimension… wherever that might be!"

Tina began drawing a picture of a polar bear after observing that the project contained facts about them. Chucky picked up some modeling clay, placed there to make a model for the little diorama that someone had already begun. The diorama represented the polar bear's natural habitat. Taking a seat, he became absorbed in making the model. He focused all of his attention on the creation of the little bear. Suddenly he felt very sleepy and it became more and more difficult to concentrate. He closed his eyes and rubbed his brow to try to wake himself up. Opening his eyes he found he had slipped into a different location. He looked around for Tina and the children who were nowhere to be found and he wondered if he had slipped into yet a different dimension or parallel universe.

This scene before him was largely unfamiliar except for some of the details. He looked around carefully, attempting to place his surroundings. He thought he might have been here before but he did not recognize it fully. He focused on the little box diorama that sat on the table in front of him, then looked up. He noticed the walls of the room were painted exactly as the walls within the box diorama. He set the completed model of the polar bear down within the diorama and instantly became aware of an object appearing next to him. It was a life-sized model of the miniature he had just built! One instant it wasn't there and the next, there it was! This startled him a little bit but Chucky put his fear aside, stood up and walked around the large bear. He marveled at how completely it resembled the miniature he had built.

As if that were not strange enough, when he put his hand on the life-sized model, his hand went right through it and disappeared. He quickly pulled his hand out and gently pressed it into the model again, this time letting his hand and arm disappear. It felt cool and he sensed some slight air currents within the emptiness inside of the model. He wondered what would happen if he were to step through the model bear. He imagined he would simply emerge out of the other side of the bear but something seemed to be pushing him to try it anyway.

He stepped forward and when half of his body was directly within the center of the model bear his surroundings changed dramatically. He realized he was moving within the bear and when he looked down at his feet he was startled at the sight of big hairy white feet moving under him. "What! What... am I the bear now?" he said out loud – or at least he thought he did!

He reached up to feel where his head should be and felt the massive face of a bear with what he imagined was his newly-acquired paw. He looked around at his surroundings and decided to move around to see what it felt like to be a bear. He wasn't particularly concerned, mainly because Marguerite had explained how he could be more than one thing at a time, past, present and future. Since he had apparently already been a cat and had remained himself at the same time, he wasn't at all worried that he wouldn't again return to himself as Chucky, the boy. He figured he might as well enjoy the experience until he figured out how to go back to being himself. He sniffed around the little fake environment and before he had a chance to move from one side of the space to the other he felt a breeze. Looking up to see the sky, it loomed massively overhead. He realized the space had been expanding and had become the real Arctic environment in which a polar bear was supposed to live. He marveled at the way things just took shape in front of him with no logical step-by-step process. Things just *became.* "That might take a little getting used to," he said to himself, or maybe out loud; he couldn't tell.

He wandered around on all fours the way a bear usually does and when he came to the edge of the floating ice he had been exploring he slipped gracefully into the cold Arctic water. It felt cool to his skin yet surprisingly not very wet. He remembered studying how polar bears had such a thick, multilayer coat that they didn't feel the cold or even wet through and through. After swimming around for a while he climbed back out. He plopped down on the ice, rolling onto his back, moving across the ice, twitching back and forth to scratch his back. He then stood up and shook off the water and ice particles beginning from his head then moving the shake all the way along his body to his tail.

He was just pondering the fact that he had a tail and that it seemed he had always had one when he heard, "Chucky! What are you doing in there?" from above him. He looked up and saw a giant Tina looking down at him. He looked around quickly and noticed he was within the diorama box where he had started. He looked down at his body and recognized himself once again as the boy he knew so well, only smaller. So small, in fact, that he was smaller than the bear model he had made for the project.

"I don't know how I got in here, actually," he said calmly as he looked around for an escape.

"Well, come back out of there," Tina whispered insistently.

It was then that he noticed the group of other faces appearing above him at the rim of the box. One of the girls he knew as Cecily in his real class gasped. "Mrs. Finkle, come quick! Chucky has stepped into his project. We're not allowed to do that, are we?" she asked in a whiny voice. "If he's allowed to do that I want to go into my turtle world project then! No fair!" she complained.

Mrs. Finkle came over to the box and peered in at the miniature Chucky. "Now, Chucky! You know better than that! You're only allowed to step in when everyone has completed their part of the project and you are only to go in with a partner. No shrinking on your own! Now come out of there!" she scolded.

Chucky immediately thought he would gladly do that if he only knew how to! He tried to remember exactly what he had done to get in there but couldn't remember anything except closing his eyes and rubbing his head. He tried it again but nothing happened.

"Uh, Mrs. Finkle... I, uh... can't get out..." he admitted.

"Oh, for Pete's sake, Chucky! Come on. Just *think* yourself out. It's not like you haven't done this one hundred times before!"

Chucky closed his eyes and imagined himself standing next to Tina and looking into the diorama box. When he opened his eyes he found himself exactly as he had imagined.

"Okay now everyone, let's get back to work," Mrs. Finkle said, walking away while giving Chucky a frown and shaking her head.

"Wow!" he whispered to Tina. "That was amazing! I think this is a parallel universe but I went into another dimension even inside this place or parallel universe... or whatever it is! I wonder how deep we can go?"

"You would be surprised," he heard Marguerite's voice say.

"Did you hear that, Tina?" he asked.

"Yes, I did. I wonder if anyone else can," she whispered back. They looked around and saw no one else paying any attention.

"They can't hear me right now," explained Marguerite. "I want you to think about something: if you can imagine this, think about how many possibilities there are. There are unlimited possibilities, infinite possibilities. You experienced going *three-deep,* as we like to call it. That is you came from your reality dimension, that's one; to a parallel universe, that's two; and into another dimension where you experienced being a bear, that's three. Now imagine going deeper. Imagine being the water the bear swam in, the molecule making up the water, the sub-atomic particle making up the water, the wave making the potential sub-atomic particle... you get what I mean, right?" Marguerite asked.

"Yeah, I think so. Then what if when I was in the wave potential I became the particle that was part of the air around me?" Chucky imagined out loud looking at the space around him.

"You have got it indeed, Chucky. Endless! Absolutely endless!" Marguerite's voice said. She had still not become visible.

"Wow, Chucky! You were a bear? When did you do that?" Tina asked.

"I don't know. I guess I was the bear at the same time I was me... I don't know," he answered, trying to figure it out.

"It's not important, Chucky. Remember there is no such thing as *time* anyway. It's all the same," Marguerite reminded.

"You know what I would like to know though?" Chucky stated, looking around. "Where is this parallel universe? I mean, where do we go when we come here? Is this another dimension? Is it the same thing?"

"Does it matter, really, Chucky? Where is the *where*? Just like when is the *when*? Have you ever thought about how many stars there are in your universe? Do you know that there are more stars in your universe than grains of sand on your planet? That's a lot of stars! Now, if you want to remember really big, think about the infinite number of possible parallel universes involved in each *potential*. Getting a big idea now?" Marguerite asked letting the last question fade into quiet.

They knew she was gone but stood contemplating the hugeness of the universe – or universes. They were snapped back into the present by Marly who had come up behind them. "You guys did a great job! Wow! I'm so glad I waited for you to do the drawing and the model building! You are both so good at art!" she praised.

Chucky looked at Tina again, absolutely amazed by the compliments and cheer coming from Marly. Tina wondered if there were some trace of this Marly inside the Marly they knew in their regular universe. She thought back to the times at Camp Tarigo a few weeks earlier when she had helped Marly with her campaign. She also thought of how full of compliments Marly had been when Tina had performed the mounted shooting demonstration on the day her parents had visited. She thought there was a little glimmer of this Marly somewhere in that Marly from her universe.

"I think I would prefer to go back to our universe now, if you don't mind, Tina. Becoming a bear is enough of an adventure for one afternoon," Chucky whispered.

Tina took his hand and imagined the air thickening directly in front of them. She closed her eyes and stepped forward, pulling Chucky with her. When she opened them they were surrounded by the same whirling cloud that had engulfed them as they travelled the Lattice.

They glided along silently for a while, this time moving more slowly than they had before. "Doesn't it remind you of going through the clouds on an airplane, or maybe like walking through fog? Look how the Lattice shows through the cloud sometimes," Tina said, marveling at the movement below her feet.

"Yeah, it does. I wonder why there is a cloud around us now but not when we go to the 'other world' school. I'd like to go back there again. It's just so different than our world. More different than the place we just came from… even though I did turn into a bear… the people are the same, though," Chucky mused.

"That must have been really cool being a bear! What did it feel like?" Tina asked.

"It felt like being me, only hairy and walking on all fours!" Chucky laughed.

"You didn't feel different?"

"No, not really. That was the odd part. I did know I was in a different body, but it was still me," Chucky explained.

"It was real then; you as a bear but still you. Just another universe – another reality, I guess," Tina said, trying to wrap her mind around the difficult thought.

"So if each universe is different in some way, using a different 'potential' as Marguerite calls it, then who decides which way things will turn out? Which one is real… like real to us, I mean?" Chucky asked.

"Well, Marguerite says that we all decide together which one we will make real," Tina answered, decidedly.

Just then they felt things thicken around them and they appeared back in their classroom. They weren't sure which 'universe' they were in but when they saw Marly moving towards them scowling, they recognized their own familiar world.

"Well it's about time! I signed us up for this project ages ago and we have to get it done! You are NOT going to make me look stupid even though YOU are, Chucky! Come on, Tina. I need your help with the art work," Marly said, taking Tina's arm and leading her across the classroom.

Chucky followed behind them not actually wanting to work anywhere near Marly but not wanting Tina to have to bear Marly on her own.

"This is what I have done so far. Now I will go write more so you and Moron Boy here can do the drawings and models," Marly said, nastily moving back to her seat.

Chucky and Tina realized the project looked exactly as it had in the parallel universe, including the modeling clay, ready for Chucky's creation.

"Wow, this is weird," Chucky stated, looking at the diorama he had just been a part of a short time before. "Too bad Marly wouldn't go 'three deep' and get eaten by another bear!"

Chapter 9

Tina spent the afternoon working on the drawings for the polar bear project in her own world making comparisons between her world and the one she had visited earlier in the day. The school had been almost identical and the people had seemed the same, other than Marly, of course.

The rest of the school day passed uneventfully and Tina, Chucky and Polly met up again later at the barn to ride Dancer, Cruiser and Toby together for the first time. After they had all three horses tacked and ready for the ride, they found the easiest path to follow around the edge of the woods, then raced each other at a canter across the field beyond. Tina would have been happy to do a full gallop with Dancer but knew that Polly and Chucky weren't as experienced yet. After a long race the three horses and riders gathered around a little pond and dropped the reins, allowing the horses to take long gulps of fresh water before letting them quietly munch the grass.

Tina had explained the day's events to Polly already before the ride, so now Polly was pressing Tina for more details about Marly in the parallel universe. "So what was she like exactly?"

"She was nothing like herself!" Chucky answered, forcefully. "She was actually nice. Can you imagine that? Marly, actually *nice?*"

"Not really!" Polly said, quickly.

"She's not that bad. I think she is like that other Marly deep down inside," Tina added, thoughtfully.

"Tina, I want to go to the 'other world'. Can we go now? I mean with the horses and all?" Polly suggested.

"I guess so. Maybe they will want to ride with us. Let's try!" Tina answered brightly.

They moved through the thickening air that began to form around them and instantly found themselves gliding gently across the Cosmic Lattice, this time without any sign of a cloud.

They came to the 'other world' and travelled across the pasture leading to the open school but no one was there, not even the horses. Since they had ridden several times in the area they decided to venture off in the direction they often took to see if they could catch up with the others. They rode for what seemed to them like an hour but still found no one.

"Maybe they are off travelling to another world today," Polly said, as she looked around sadly.

"They might be but I have an idea. You know how everything we imagine here comes about quickly? Well, why don't we put our thoughts together on the rest of the kids coming back to us right here where we are on this path? Do you think it would work?" Tina suggested.

"Let's try," Chucky encouraged.

"Okay, let's imagine how they would look if they were coming around that bend over there. Who would be riding first?" Tina asked.

"Well, it would be Heather, for sure, then Ben, then maybe Jiankara..." Polly started.

"Let's imagine them in that order then. Heather likes to ride that Dunn mare, and Ben likes to ride Onyx when we don't, and Jiankara? Which horse does she ride?" Chucky pondered out loud.

No sooner had they begun to imagine the others coming in as much detail as they could, the children came around the bend in the exact order they had imagined.

"Wow, that was fast," Polly said, quietly amazed.

When they had all ridden up and greeted each other they set off again for another riding path forming a line of two and three horses abreast.

Tina rode next to Polly and Chucky moved slightly ahead to ride next to Ben. Mr. Pierce rode back and circled to ride up next to Tina.

"Mr. Pierce, I am wondering. Did you know that Polly, Chucky and I were thinking of you all riding to meet us?" Tina asked.

"Well, yes, we did. We all felt your thoughts on us and we knew, as a group, that we should take that specific path to meet you. Here we are trained starting when we are very little to sense when someone is thinking of us and if they are calling us to them," he answered.

"That is awesome!" Polly said excitedly. "I wish *I* could do that!"

"You can learn to, Polly. It is a very handy thing to know how to do. It takes a great deal of practice in your world though because the whole group, most everybody on Earth, doesn't think it can be done. You've been told before what everyone thinks is what becomes real, right?" Mr. Pierce inquired.

"Yes, I understand that, but how do I get everyone to think about things they don't think are real so they can become real?" Polly asked, thoughtfully.

"Well, that's a good point but you might or might not be able to do that. You can slowly change the way people see things by giving them an example of what it looks like to be different. A famous man once said, "Be the change you want to see." An example of this could mean simply that you always find a parking spot for your mother when you are with her by creating it first in your mind. When you practice this enough you will see you can make it appear every time. When people see you do this often enough they will begin to believe that you can do that. Eventually others will try it too and before you know it being able to create a parking space will become commonly accepted and no one will even remember a time when very few people could do it!" Mr. Pierce said, smiling broadly at the thought.

"I'm going to try that," Tina said.

"That is just a little example but there are many more important changes you can make," Mr. Pierce continued. "Here on this world we have an idea about what all of you are up to on your planet. We think that is the exact reason you have decided to live in your world with the way things are. You actually want to make great changes."

"We do? How would we do that?" Tina asked, trying to imagine how hard it would be to change a whole world.

"Almost everybody in your world would like to see things be a little bit better. Most people want to be happier and healthier; wouldn't you say that is true?"

"Well, yes, I guess so," Tina answered.

"The only trouble is while they are there they have forgotten who they really are. They are really great wizards with the power to change anything. But you know that, don't you, Tina?" Marguerite said, materializing on horseback next to Polly and Tina.

"Oh! Hi, Marguerite. Yes, I remember your telling me that before," Tina answered, surprised.

Chucky dropped back to rejoin Tina and Polly, not wanting to miss the rest of the conversation. "Hi, Marguerite."

"Hi, Chucky," Marguerite greeted, smiling broadly. "The great thing is that the people of your world are losing patience with themselves, but the only way they will be able to change things is by remembering who they are and by using their full potential. You can help them by seeing them for who they really are beneath the surface. After all, remember that we are all the same thing! Just fast moving wave potential!"

The children smiled at that reminder and Tina added, "Yeah! Even Marly!"

"That's right, Tina. As difficult as it is to see sometimes, Marly is a part of you, too, just as you have imagined," Marguerite agreed.

Heather circled back to join the group and offer her opinion, "I think Marly is funny! She tries to act so uncaring but she is really interested in everything here in this world. I hope she will come back one day."

"I doubt she will," Chucky stated, flatly.

"She might, Chucky! She just needs a little more time to remember who she really is. I'm going to keep trying to remind her in little ways without saying much directly. I am going to give her chances to show me the parts of her I like the best and try to ignore the parts I don't, like I always do. Then I think if we all keep focused on her being nicer she will seem that way to us. Do you think that will work?" Tina asked, directing her question to Marguerite.

"It is certainly worth a try!" the angel answered, brightly.

After they had ridden for some time, Chucky picked up on some of the horses' thoughts of hunger and suggested that the group turn back to the grazing pasture. Cruiser had seemed to enjoy the 'other world' and made Chucky feel confident and comfortable on his back.

They made their way back to the open schoolroom and let the horses roam and nibble the grass until Aiden brought a couple of fresh hay bales out for them to do some more serious eating.

Continuing their earlier conversation, Polly looked at Marguerite and asked, "You know, it seems to me that people are not very happy in our world. I understand that they have forgotten who they are but it's too hard to remember when everything is… well… so mixed up!"

"Certainly it is!" Marguerite confirmed. "But there are a few things you can do to remind yourself. One of the most important ways to feel happier is to avoid basing happiness on whether or not anything changes in the world. You might be looking for things to change but you should feel happiness regardless if it does or not!"

"Well, what if you don't like the way things are?" Polly asked, whining a little.

"Polly, no matter what has happened to you in life you are not your story. Every single day you have the opportunity to recreate yourself exactly as you want to be *this* day!" Marguerite encouraged.

"How can I do that? How can I be all happy if everything keeps happening to me every day?" Polly whined.

"Children," Marguerite directed at Polly, Chucky and Tina, "Polly has brought up a really good question and I will give you the answer, but it is going to take some thinking on your part to understand deep down inside. This truth is almost the biggest secret in the universe."

The children drew in a little closer and waited anxiously for Marguerite to reveal the secret. After smiling and admiring the children paying such close attention she continued, "Nothing is happening to you outside of you. You are making it all up. What is happening *is* happening, but *how* you are experiencing what is happening is being completely made up by you!"

No one said a word. Each wanted to avoid appearing confused since it was supposed to be an important secret.

"You have all come very far in your understanding of the way the universe works," Marguerite continued. "You now understand how we create everything by intentionally collapsing wave potentials into particles, right?" The children nodded in agreement. "Well, you also know that you yourselves and all of your thoughts are vibrations too, yes?" The children nodded in agreement once again.

"The greater part of you, that higher self we have talked about, thought *you* into being the physical *you*. This is so you could experience the universe. Everybody has done that! Everybody has a larger part of themselves, all connected, as we have also talked about. So you are all like magicians watching your own magic tricks – your illusions! And you are doing it all together, each person creating his or her own play and everybody else is an actor or an actress in it," Marguerite explained excitedly.

"I get it," Tina said, realizing what Marguerite meant. "We live in the make believe, but it is *us* who is doing that, not someone else. Only thing is, when we're in the middle of it, it seems so real."

"Yes, but if you keep reminding yourself that it is *you* putting people and situations in your path, like gifts. These gifts will let you grow and remember who you really are! You are a perfect magician wanting to know yourself as, well, whatever it is you create. That could be knowing yourself as brave, loving, intelligent and forgiving; any number of qualities you might want to be," Marguerite explained.

"You can see things taking shape in front of you, yet you don't have to get caught up in it as if it is an act in a play you are in. In a play most of the characters are not in every scene. Furthermore, some have speaking parts and some might be observing the scene. You can be like the actor who is just observing but not fully participating. How you do that in real life is by deciding how you *feel* and then deciding what to do about how you feel. That's it," Marguerite said.

"So we are writing our play as we are going along?" Chucky asked, trying to get a picture in his mind of himself as a magician writing a story.

"Yes, Chucky, exactly. With the endless potentials you are writing it and living it at the same time," Marguerite confirmed.

"Then why does it feel like someone else is writing it and I am living it?" Polly asked.

"It seems that way so you can have the delight of discovering things as you go along. It would be boring if you knew the outcome of the story, wouldn't it?" Marguerite asked.

"Well, yeah, I guess so," Polly answered, sounding unsure.

"The bigger *you* is commanding the ship, Polly. You are participating by being the actor and you know part of the story but not the whole thing. A little bit becomes clear to you at a time. It's more fun that way and you and your higher self together have an opportunity to change the course of things along the way," Marguerite explained.

"Then why doesn't everybody know this? Why don't grownups know this?" Chucky asked.

"It is there for everyone to discover but most everyone comes into your world having forgotten about it to give themselves the joy in discovering the big secret!" Marguerite exclaimed.

"I'll bet nobody would believe it if you told them in our world anyway," Chucky said.

"We're just luckier than most of the people in our world because we have been to this one and we have learned lots about how the universe works here," Tina said.

"Yes, you have and you can come back here anytime to learn more," Mr. Pierce said, having listened quietly until now.

"If everybody could come here and do the things we have done they would get to know how the universe works, too!" Polly added, cheerfully.

"Yeah, but who wants them? And anyway, look at Marly. She came here and still doesn't believe anything," Chucky said, thinking how Marly had behaved.

"Marly is just in her own way for now and maybe everyone doesn't need to discover the secret in the same way," Jiankara interjected.

"Maybe it's no fun for some people to learn it. Maybe some people want to keep it like it is," Polly said, thoughtfully.

"That's right, Polly. We choose for ourselves all along the way," Marguerite reminded.

"I'm hungry!" Ben interrupted. "Can we eat now?"

"So am I!" said Heather, moving towards the baskets that had been set up in the open school building. She motioned for the others to follow.

Marguerite took the opportunity to wish the children farewell, and vanished, smiling and waving. The children all took a basket and sat at the edge of the open classroom, letting their feet dangle over the edge of the raised step.

After Chucky had taken his seat, Heather squeezed in between him and Polly, making Chucky feel a little bit uncomfortable. "Are you going to come here often, Chucky? Why don't you come to school here every day?" she asked. "That way you can be my boyfriend!"

"Heather! Leave him alone," Ben urged. "You'll scare him away for good!"

"You aren't scared of me, are you, Chucky?" Heather asked, boldly.

"Uh… no… I… uh…" Chucky stammered embarrassed.

Polly giggled and said, "We'll come here often but I'm going to go to school in my world, too. You too, Chucky?"

Chucky was grateful at the chance to agree with Polly's suggestion so he wouldn't have to get further into the conversation with Heather. "Yes! I will come with you and Tina, too… often… very often."

"We need to stay in our world to go to school some of the time because we have to learn to be like others there… only with a whole lot more information. How else would we be the examples of how to… well, how to be?" Tina asked, not really expecting an answer.

The children continued talking about the differences and similarities between their worlds, eating slowly and happily. They stayed until late in the evening, then rode quietly back and across the Lattice, reaching the barn exactly when they had left. Thoroughly tired out, they all agreed to head home after untacking and getting the horses settled in Cruiser's new pasture. Even the horses wandered off slowly to doze in the late afternoon sunlight.

Chapter 10

A few days later, Tina brought Dancer out to ride using only a halter and lead rope. She loved to glide along with Dancer; sometimes she would lie out along her back and rest her head on the horse's neck while letting her arms and legs hang loosely around Dancer's shoulders and belly. Tina pretended she were a rag doll carefully placed on a stuffed animal horse and imagined a giant holding them, and playing that they were riding along an imaginary landscape.

After some time, Tina slid to the ground to let Dancer graze quietly while she made her way towards a big tree where she could sit and watch Dancer. She never tired of watching her horse. Dancer had been her closest companion for several years now and she was delighted to be able to hear direct feelings and intentions from her horse. She still couldn't hear words like Chucky could, but every day she was learning to sense more and more.

Tina leaned back against the tree and closed her eyes. She felt tremendous gratitude for everything that made her world so happy. She wasn't thinking about each and every thing, but rather the whole of it together. Life, she decided, was good!

She took a deep breath and let her mind begin to drift through her 'mind garden' like she had learned to do in the 'other world' school. She took note of the flowers she passed along her imaginary path until she reached what she figured might be a grandmother tree since it had several pieces of brightly colored paper hanging from the limbs. As if by instinct alone she knew which papers to pluck from the tree because these were the ones that held her personal messages. After pocketing them, she made her way inside the little door at the base of the trunk. The door was so tiny Tina had to make herself as small as possible to squeeze through it.

Entering one of the tree's corridors, Tina walked along until she found an open door. She peeked inside to see if anyone was there and she saw a tall woman standing near the window.

"Come in, Tina. What questions do you have for me?" the woman asked.

Tina sensed this woman was very wise like her own angel, Marguerite, but she didn't think this woman was an angel. Perhaps it was her eyes, the way they gazed knowingly at Tina, as if she had known her through lifetimes. She didn't glow like an angel, or even seem 'real but angelic' the way Sequoia had when she had first met her at summer camp just a few weeks earlier. The woman seemed very familiar however. Tina reached into her pocket and withdrew one of the papers she had plucked from the tree.

"Uh… hello… uh," she stuttered. She looked down at the paper and read aloud, "Why are we here?"

The woman smiled and Tina thought they must be related to each other because this woman looked a great deal like a family member. Tina still couldn't place who she was.

"We are here, Tina, to continue with the great experiment of Earth," the woman answered slowly.

"Experiment? What experiment?" Tina asked.

"We are here to see if light can win over dark; if the universe can keep expanding ever outward; and if we can raise our vibrations so high they reach the highest state of all. That vibration is unconditional love. When we raise the frequency of our vibration, we experience unconditional love," she explained.

Tina stood quietly for a moment considering what the woman might have meant about expanding and vibration. She thought about what she had learned at the 'other world' school about everything being a vibration, energy in motion. She also remembered that thoughts and feelings themselves were merely a vibration so that might make thoughts become real things.

"Do you mean we are here to make thoughts into physical things?" Tina asked.

"Yes, and in doing that you help everything in the universe expand. Through greater understanding of your experiences you raise your vibrations and everything else's. This is done through thoughts and actions into creation," the woman answered. "As you think and feel, shift vibrations of yourself, and in so doing, you will affect things around you. You can create - mindfulness to manifesting – thoughts to creation."

Tina took another of the papers from her pocket and read, "How do we get to that highest vibration?"

"First, take the focus off of yourself. Only seek knowledge about how to make positive changes in yourself so you can show others to do it, not to try to be better than anyone else. Be the change you would like to see in others. That can mean showing patience, compassion, generosity, honesty and mindfulness. You are quite a good example of those traits, Tina. Next, seek to understand the importance of love. That doesn't mean you have to like everybody, but it means you should feel some level of love for them or some level of appreciation for them. Think how you feel about your grandmother. You don't like her very much, but you actually feel love for her, don't you?" the woman asked.

"Yes, I do. I guess I forgive her for being unlikeable and actually love her, even though I don't like her all of the time," Tina answered.

The woman smiled, and continued, "Replace every angry thought with one of love. While anger can arise even at someone you love, let it pass and refocus on the love you truly feel. Just as you do with your grandmother. Learn to love more. Learn to forgive all and love everyone unconditionally. Learn that we are all loved. This will make the world, and then, in turn, the universe, a better place to be and expand it to the next best potential!" the woman said. She spoke very slowly as if considering the weight of every word.

Tina understood what the woman was talking about since Marguerite had explained about the infinite number of potentials and possibilities before. Preparing to leave, thinking this was all the woman had to say to her, Tina turned towards the door, bowing her head politely.

"Don't you have one more question, Tina?" the woman asked.

Tina reached into her pocket and took out another paper and read, "Who are you?"

"I am *you*, Tina," she stated, smiling broadly.

Tina looked at the woman and recognized that this woman could be exactly as Tina herself would appear in another twenty years. She smiled, nodded gratefully and left the Grandmother Tree. She wandered through her mind garden until she reached the tree where she had begun her journey. Tina opened her eyes, looked around and saw Dancer peacefully grazing a few yards away from her. She got up to collect Dancer and head back to the barn, reaching into her pocket to find the sugar cube she had brought as a treat for her. As she pulled it out, a few little colored pieces of paper gently drifted onto the grass. Tina bent down to pick them up but was only able to get one. A swift breeze came suddenly and swept up the rest, taking them far out of reach. She unfolded the one she had recovered expecting another question to be written on it, but it was blank. Tina imagined the messages could only be seen at the Grandmother Tree.

~~~~~~

"We were just having a discussion with Marly here, Tina," Polly said, sounding a little bit frustrated.

"As usual she won't listen," Chucky groused.

"I *am* listening, but no one making any sense is talking!" Marly shot back.

"What's the discussion about?" Tina asked, not directing her question at any one of them in particular.

"They have been trying to convince me that the crazy phony place you three go off to all the time is real. I know you must have played a trick on me that day. It wasn't real!" Marly stated almost angrily.

"Well if it wasn't real, Marly, how is it that we made everyone freeze before we left?" Tina asked. She couldn't believe that Marly really thought everything was just a trick, but she realized that perhaps Marly was afraid to admit the world they were experiencing was a safer one and she preferred to feel safe. After all, she thought, some people are just not cut out to be pioneers. Learning and incorporating what we have learned in the 'other world' school here in our world sure makes us like pioneers!

Marly considered for a minute and then shrugged her shoulders. "And then how did we make the Cosmic Lattice happen? For that matter, how did we make Marguerite float on the Cosmic Lattice?" Tina queried further.

"I don't know how you did all that but anyway it wasn't a real school when we got there, was it? They didn't have any books or things to write with…" Marly said.

Chucky cut her off before she could say anything else. "So you admit you don't know how we made it all up but you do admit you did go somewhere, right?"

"Well, yeah, so maybe we did…so what? Maybe we went somewhere but it wasn't a school!" Marly shot back defensively.

Tina looked Marly directly in the eyes and thought about what the woman, herself as an adult, had said, "Learn to forgive and love everyone unconditionally." She recognized that she did love Marly even as she was. It didn't matter that for some reason, deep inside, Marly wasn't able to believe something so amazing as the 'other world' yet. Tina forgave her. She thought Marly just wasn't ready for a new world, probably because her parents weren't, and if Marly told her parents about the 'other world' they simply wouldn't believe her. Tina knew that to Marly, pleasing her parents was the most important thing in the world. If that included pretending something important didn't exist, well, she thought, that was just the way Marly had decided it should be.

"We did go somewhere though, right?" Tina asked softly.

"Yeah," Marly answered, lowering her tone to match Tina's.

"And it was kind of fun, wasn't it?" Tina asked encouragingly. Marly thought for a moment and then nodded in agreement.

"Well, that's a start," Tina said, smiling at Marly, then turning to Chucky, who rolled his eyes but smiled in spite of himself. Polly too was beaming and giggled at Chucky rolling his eyes.

About the Author:

Kimberly Wickham holds an MA in Humanities and has over twenty years experience teaching visual and performing arts, gifted and talented programs, troubled youth and economics.

Kimberly currently travels extensively discussing her books and philosophy for children while continuing to write and study Meta & Quantum physics.

http://www.kimberlywickham.com